Parents & Teachers Working Together

Carol Davis
Alice Yang

Introduction by Roxann Kriete

STRATEGIES FOR TEACHERS SERIES

The stories in this book are all based on real events in the classroom. However, in order to respect the privacy of students, names and many identifying characteristics of students and situations have been changed.

ISBN: 978-1-892989-15-4
Library of Congress control number 2005921576

Photographs: Peter Wrenn

Cover and book design: Woodward Design

NORTHEAST FOUNDATION FOR CHILDREN
85 Avenue A, Suite 204
P.O. Box 718
Turners Falls, MA 01376-0718
800-360-6332

www.responsiveclassroom.org

14 13 12 11 10   8 7 6 5 4

We would like to thank the Shinnyo-en Foundation for its generous support of the development of this book.

The mission of the Shinnyo-en Foundation is "to bring forth deeper compassion among humankind, to promote greater harmony, and to nurture future generations toward building more caring communities."

ACKNOWLEDGMENTS

Lots of people put lots of hours into this book. They range from the staff at Northeast Foundation for Children to classroom teachers in many states. They include parents of elementary age students and elementary students themselves. Directly and indirectly, all these people's ideas, stories, and suggestions made this book possible. We're deeply grateful to all of them. In particular, we'd like to thank the following people:

Mary Beth Forton, associate director of NEFC, for believing in us and for guiding the development of this book with extraordinary wisdom and care. Her suggestions were always gentle and on target, and she was always willing to talk through a problem or read through a draft.

Roxann Kriete, executive director of NEFC, for writing the introduction, supplying key framing of the last chapter of this book, and reading the manuscript.

Colleagues affiliated with NEFC who helped with early conceptualization of the book, shared stories, put us in touch with teachers, read the manuscript, helped secure funding for this book, or served as another set of eyes to check for accuracy and consistency: *Adam Berkin, Marcia Bradley, Kathryn Brady, Carolyn Bush, Ruth Sidney Charney, Marlynn Clayton, Linda Crawford, Paula Denton, Jay Lord, Elizabeth Nash, Sue Rosa, Bonnie Baer-Simahk,* and *Chip Wood.*

Editorial Advisory Board members *Caltha Crowe, Sharon Dunn, Karen Latka,* and *Clement Seldin,* who offered the fresh perspectives that helped us make the book useful for teachers in a variety of educational settings. Clement additionally served as a manuscript reader.

Ramona McCullough for gathering so many sample letters and forms and modeling ways to reach out to *all* parents.

The parents, teachers, and principals whose stories of school-home collaboration informed this book's content. In addition to people named in the book, we'd like to thank *Beth Allen, Greg Bagley, Cindy Benner, Karen Casto, Joann Deacon, Andy Dousis, Rick Ellis, Pat Fekete, Sue Hartmann, Adair Heitmann, Mary Beth Hilborn, Connie Kissam, Mary Ellen Lane, Patty Lawrence, Bekki Lee, Jodi McErlane, Mary Mirecki, Kerry O'Grady, Sarae Pacetta, Melissa Porter, Bethany Robinson, Gail Sperling, Wilson Soto, Patty Stegman, Raysa Vidal,* and *Rosetta Wilson.*

The teachers, administrators, and children at *Hart Magnet School* in Stamford, Connecticut; *Six to Six Interdistrict Magnet School* in Bridgeport, Connecticut; and

Regional Multicultural Magnet School in New London, Connecticut, for welcoming us into their schools to observe and take photographs.

Janice Gadaire Fleuriel, proofreader, for handling this job with her hallmark efficiency and cheeriness.

Photographer *Peter Wrenn* for supplying so many excellent photos for this book. His commitment to quality is an inspiration.

Leslie and *Jeff Woodward,* graphic designers, for again transforming a bundle of papers into a finished book that is both beautiful and easy to use.

Additional Acknowledgments

I would like to thank my colleagues and friends at NEFC—*Susan Roser, Sally Kitts,* and *Eileen Mariani* in addition to the individuals named above—and at Summit Elementary School, in particular *Jean Schweickart,* my mentor, teaching partner, and dear friend. I am also grateful for the wisdom, love, and support of my siblings, *Anne, Rusty,* and *John;* and my parents, *Larry* and *Honey Hofmann.* I would like to thank my daughter, *Riley,* for teaching me all the important things I know about being a good parent. Thank you for sharing your mommy while I wrote this book. Finally, I wish to thank my husband, *Timothy,* for listening and cheering me on as I agonized over every word. I could not have written this book without your love and support. —*Carol Davis*

I wish to thank my partner, *Janet,* for always being there with a most helpful blend of loving support and practical suggestions. Thanks, also, for your research help. I'm also grateful to my parents, siblings, and mentors along the way for instilling in me the importance of education along with deep respect for teachers and the teaching profession. —*Alice Yang*

TABLE OF CONTENTS

Notes to Our Readers

The term "parent"

In this book we use the term "parent" to mean any adult who is the child's primary caregiver: mother, father, grandmother, grandfather, other relative, or other legal guardian. We recognize the diversity in family structures and the challenge of coming up with one word that fits all situations. Our intention in using the word "parent" is to honor all those who devote their time, attention, care, and love to raising children.

The "I" in this book

While this book has two authors, the "I" throughout the text refers to Carol Davis. The stories and insights told in this first-person voice are Carol's and are gleaned from her extensive experience as a classroom teacher and a *Responsive Classroom*® consultant.

Introduction

OPENING THE DOOR TO FAMILIES

By Roxann Kriete,
executive director of Northeast Foundation for Children

When my oldest child entered kindergarten twenty years ago, I remember pulling an envelope from his school out of our mailbox one warm August day. The letter not only welcomed him but also welcomed my husband and me "as partners" in his education. We were pleased by the acknowledgment.

But as a teacher myself, I was also aware of how much easier it is to name such a partnership than to live in one. "Partners." The word lingered in my mind. I thought about other kinds of partnerships that I was familiar with, both business and personal. Partnering with someone involves a serious commitment. What kind of partnership exactly was this going to be? I wondered. What would the balance of power be in it? What were the roles and responsibilities of each member? What would happen when conflicts arose?

As a teacher, I had often asked myself the same questions about school-home partnerships. Now, however, I was for the first time on the parent end of the relationship. The difference in perspective was enlightening. As a teacher, I knew that at the heart of all my questions about the school-home partnership was the question of trust. For this partnership to go well, great trust is required: Teachers must trust parents, and parents must trust teachers. But as a parent, I was now experiencing firsthand just how profoundly parents are asked to trust. They're asked to trust not only a particular teacher in a particular year, but also the institution of school—all the teachers and all the years of school that their child will experience. Between kindergarten and fifth grade, a standard elementary school span, a child spends over a thousand days in school. What an influence the people and the culture of the school will have!

My son's kindergarten year passed. In both his and his younger sister's elementary years, there were many wonderful teachers who took care to build good relationships with our family. Though I cannot claim that I found answers to all my questions about school-home partnerships—they are, after all, big questions without simple answers—our family did experience many instances of respectful, fruitful collaboration with teachers. It's now twenty years later. These intervening two decades have provided me with many experiences, observations, and conversations as a parent and educator with parents and educators. I have gained some insights into the issue of teachers and parents working together, and I also have new questions. Some of these have to do with the growing diversity of our population, which has made the terrain more varied, more interesting, and more challenging than ever.

**The critical
role of
teachers**

Yet while my list of questions has grown, so has my conviction about the vital importance of the school-family partnership. Children flourish best when there is respect and cooperation among the adults who care for them at home and at school. The value to students of open communication and a good working relationship between school and home is clear. Experience and common sense suggest it; research confirms it. (See box on page 7.)

The critical role of teachers

In the work of cultivating a positive relationship between home and school, teachers play a critical role. Their actions and words, how well they listen to parents, and how genuinely they respect families deeply affect how much trust there will be between parent and teacher. Not only that, but as families' most immediate contact with the school, teachers can make a significant difference in how much families trust the institution of school. I don't mean to imply that it's up to individual teachers to tend to relationships between families and the school as a whole. That work is shared by school principals, home liaisons, and other staff. What I am asserting is that individual teachers have great power in influencing families' feelings about school as an institution. The rewards of a good teacher-parent working relationship can often be felt well beyond the classroom walls.

Yet if the rewards are great, so can be the challenges for both teachers and parents. Unlike most adult partnership arrangements, there is little choice involved in the pairing of teachers and parents. These partnerships are usually announced via class lists—lists informed by geography, date of birth, the alphabet, gender ratios, and assorted other factors. And, parents and teachers both come with a set of experiences and assumptions about learning and children and homes and schooling. Those sets may be very aligned or quite divergent.

Fortunately, no matter what differences exist, both parents and teachers bring deep caring and commitment to the growth and success of the children. Once children enter school, their education and development become a joint project of home and school, and both teachers and parents have critical areas of expertise to contribute. Teachers know child development, curriculum, and methods that help children learn. They are experienced at helping children work and share in groups. Parents are experts on their particular children—how they naturally take in information, what energizes and delights them, what they do when they stumble, how they show that they are upset, and what comforts them when they are worried.

The five "eyes"

So how can teachers help ensure that this joint project is successful? In my early days as a teacher I asked a mentor of mine how to increase teacher-parent collaboration in a school project. Though she had learned it from her days as a fundraiser, her answer offers wisdom for any situation where shared investment is a goal. "Remember the five eyes," she said.

The five eyes. It sounded profound—at least a little mythical. I nodded. Should I confess that I had no idea what she was talking about? I ran through the mythical creatures I could summon up in my mind's one eye. Cyclops? Gorgon? Medusa? "The five eyes," I said thoughtfully, stalling for time.

"You know: Identify, Inform, Invite, Involve, Invest." Aha. She was talking I's, not eyes. She went on. "First you have to identify the common interest, then you have to make sure they have information about it, invite them to be a part of it in meaningful ways, involve them when they accept that invitation. Do all that, and there'll be investment."

The strategies in this book

In *Parents and Teachers Working Together* the authors offer a wealth of strategies that identify common goals among parent, teacher, and child; that inform parents; that invite them into the life of the classroom and the school; and that involve them in ways which encourage investment in successful collaboration.

Three things stand out about the strategies in this book. First, they are practical. There are specific, do-able suggestions for ways to inform parents, from weekly work folders sent home to postcards mailed a few times a year. There are ideas for how to ask parents for information, such as through holding goal-naming conferences and leaving spaces for parents' comments in papers sent home. There are sample letters and forms, as well as sample language to use when talking with parents.

Second, the strategies offered are two-directional. By that I mean they're not just about how teachers can get information to parents; they're also about how teachers can hear *from* parents about their hopes and concerns, receiving *from* them their insights and wisdom. The strategies also aren't just about how teachers can get parents to support the curriculum or support classroom life; they're about how parents' interests, skills, and insights can infuse the curriculum and classroom life. We often hear that parents should have an *active* role in their children's education. This book gives specific ideas for turning that ideal into reality.

Third, this book allows teachers to go at their own pace and to pick and choose. The strategies offered work well together but do not have to be implemented all at once to be effective. In fact, for most of us, launching too many new projects at once is just overwhelming. Far better to try a couple of changes, evaluate how they're working, and refine them before adding more. Some readers may decide that a certain strategy simply doesn't work for their particular situation. They may want to change it significantly or abandon it altogether.

The strategies in this book

Security work

Security work

There's a lot of attention these days—sadly and rightly so—on issues of the physical security of schools. In some cases sentries are posted to screen visitors, keeping the school community safe by ensuring that only the "right" people enter.

Teachers also stand, literally and metaphorically, at our classroom and schoolhouse doors. But instead of blocking intruders, they open their doors often and widely, greeting and welcoming their students and their families. They teach their children to greet one another in many languages and invite parents into the classroom greeting activities as well. They make sure that the pictures on the walls and the books on the shelves reflect the situations of the children they teach. They send emails and newsletters and invite parents to observe and to participate. The atmosphere that is created by their engagement with parents in so many ways—in both everyday and crisis interactions—is security work as well. It's work that makes school safe, joyful, and full of learning.

Yes, teachers do occupy a position at the doorways to children's education. And it's such a critical post.

What Research Says about Parent Involvement

- Regardless of family income or background, students whose parents are involved in their schooling are more likely to have higher grades and test scores, attend school regularly, have better social skills, show improved behavior, and adapt well to school. (Henderson and Mapp 2002)

- The most accurate predictors of student achievement in school are not family income or social status, but the extent to which the family creates a home environment that encourages learning, communicates high yet reasonable expectations for the child's achievement, and becomes involved in the child's education at school. (National PTA 2000, 11-12)

- When parents are involved at school, the performance of all the children at school, not just their own, tends to improve. (Henderson and Berla 1995, 14-16)

- The more comprehensive and well planned the partnership between school and home, the higher the student achievement. (Henderson and Berla 1995, 14-16)

Introduction

Chapter One

WORKING WITH FAMILIES OF DIFFERENT CULTURES

The teacher talking with us about our family's culture and how it can be supported in the classroom. Listening without assumptions. Representations of many cultures on the classroom walls. Assignments that incorporate voices from many U.S. cultures. All these help reassure me that our family's culture is respected and valued in my child's classroom.

Parent of a second grader

One of the enduring truths about teaching which so many educators have learned is that in order to teach children well, we have to know them. We have to know them as individuals: what they're passionate about, what they're good at, what worries them. We have to understand where they are in their cognitive, social, language, and physical development. And, importantly, we have to understand something of their family culture.

With the U.S. school-age population becoming increasingly diverse, understanding students' family cultures has become a more important and complex issue for teachers. It's always been our job as teachers to remember that students live in communities and families, and that this world outside the classroom has a huge effect on how well they do in school. But now, more than ever, we need to be attentive to how the culture of students' family and community lives can be very different from our own culture or the dominant culture of the school. And once we begin to see the differences, we need to know how to respond.

This cultural responsiveness needs to permeate everything we do with students and parents all year long. It shouldn't be an add-on, a special diversity project or multicultural celebration to be done during a particular time of the day or the year. Instead, cultural responsiveness should infuse all the topics discussed in this book, from reaching out to parents in the first weeks of school through celebrating the year with them during the last weeks of school. In this chapter, I offer some background information, some principles to keep in mind when working with students and parents across cultures, and then some practical strategies to try.

How Diverse Are We?

Just what kind of diversity are we talking about when we discuss diversity in the classroom? And how diverse are we? Some data can begin to paint the picture:

How Diverse Are We?

Hard but Exhilarating Work

- In 2002, one in four U.S. children ages five through thirteen was a child of color. (U.S. Census Bureau, June 18, 2003)

- By 2020, nearly half of all U.S. children will be of color. About one in four will be Hispanic, one in seven will be non-Hispanic Black, and one in fifteen will be Asian or Pacific Islander. (U.S. Census Bureau 2000)

- In 2000, 3.4 million U.S. children ages five through seventeen (about one in fifteen) spoke little or no English. (American Educational Research Association 2004)

- The top ten home languages spoken by U.S. students learning English in 2001 were Spanish, Vietnamese, Hmong, Chinese (Cantonese), Korean, Haitian Creole, Arabic, Russian, Tagalog, and Navajo. Nearly 400 home languages are spoken by students in the United States. (U.S. Department of Education 2000-2001)

Race, ethnicity, and language are not the only forms of diversity teachers are seeing. Families also differ in income, education level, the dialect of English spoken, and how long they've lived in the U.S. They differ in family structure as well: some children are being raised by one parent, others two; some are being raised by a grandparent or other relative; some have two moms or two dads; many children are adopted. Knowing our students and their families means being attentive and respectful of all of these differences.

Hard but Exhilarating Work

Many teachers find interacting with parents across cultures to be hard work, perhaps the hardest part of their teaching. There's no doubt it can be hard. It challenges teachers to do things a little differently. For example, teachers may need to assign different homework for children whose parents speak no English—homework that either requires no adult help or allows parents to help without using English. Working with parents of diverse cultures also challenges teachers to stretch their powers of understanding and empathy. Fairfax, Virginia, teacher Manjula Ganesh, for example, tells of listening to one recently immigrated parent complain that her child was not being taught well because the class didn't sit at rows of desks, study textbooks, memorize, or do drills the way children did in her native country. It took time and hard work for Manjula and this parent to achieve a mutual understanding of each other's goals, concerns, and educational philosophies.

But if working with parents from different cultures is hard work, it can also be exhilarating work. In her book *The Light in Their Eyes,* education professor Sonia Nieto talks about the dazzling look of discovery in students' eyes when they become excited about learning (Nieto 1999, xix). As teachers, we come into the profession because we find joy in seeing children learn, from seeing that light in their eyes. When we build bridges to families of various cultures, we increase the chances that their children, not just the children of mainstream cultures, will do well in school.

We also open up exciting new worlds of learning for *all* children when we embrace diversity in our classrooms. Just think of the social and academic growth that can happen for all students when the curriculum reflects the traditions and contributions of all cultures in the U.S. today. In a recent study of school desegregation by Teachers College and the University of California at Los Angeles, the researchers felt it was so important for children to be exposed to various cultures that they urged policy makers to consider racial diversity as one measure of a "good" public school. (Wells, Holme, Revilla, and Atanda 2004, 7)

Many parents, too, value inclusiveness in the classroom. Bekki Lee, parent of a second grader and a ninth grader, says, "To have a teacher affirm and embrace all cultures, especially those that our society most under-represents or misrepresents, is incredibly powerful." She continues, "Teachers shape how our children see the world and each other, and it is never too early to begin developing children's respectful openness to differences."

Before going any further, I want to emphasize the importance of teachers seeking help on issues of diversity. Bridging cultures is complex business. Today, as I work with teachers in various parts of the country, I am struck by how many different cultures individual teachers are in contact with. Besides often having to navigate several languages, teachers must learn about different communication etiquettes and child raising approaches. Trying to do this alone is daunting and impossible. We need to rely on colleagues and community members. Collectively, the staff of a school will know more than any single teacher can hope to. Together, a community can do a lot more than any one school ever can.

So often, teachers are reluctant to ask for help. Perhaps we fear that seeking help means somehow we're incompetent. Nothing can be further from the truth. Seeking help from a variety of sources shows that we understand the complexity of the issue and that we're willing to give it the attention and resources it deserves.

A Goal and a Belief

A Goal and a Belief

I would like to suggest one overarching goal and one fundamental belief to keep in mind as we work with families of different cultures:

The goal: Helping children learn

The goal in working with parents—all parents, no matter what their culture— is to enable them to support their children in learning. It sounds simple, but in the process of finding innovative ways to understand and include all the cultures of our students, it's sometimes easy to lose sight of this goal.

In *The Light in Their Eyes,* Sonia Nieto observes that many schools believe they're offering multicultural education when they're implementing "little more than ethnic additives and cultural celebrations." She writes, "Curiously missing from discussions in most schools that claim to 'do' multicultural education are statements having to do with *student learning.*" Nieto recalls telling a friend one day about a multicultural education initiative in a nearby school system. After hearing the details of the project, the friend asked, "But are the kids learning?" Several years later, another friend echoed this concern during a conversation about the various ways children benefit in multicultural programs. The friend asked impatiently, "But can they do math?" (Nieto 1999, xvi)

"Are the children learning?" needs to be the question that we continually keep in the forefront of our mind as we work with all parents. Celebrating holidays from various cultures, inviting parents to share something from their culture with the class, and decorating a bulletin board to reflect diverse cultures are all worthwhile activities. But we need to ask ourselves whether such efforts, by themselves, help children do the learning they're supposed to do in school.

I believe that to help children learn, we need to have practices, policies, and beliefs that allow their parents to help them learn. That means making the small but critical everyday efforts to ensure that parents are informed of classroom and school happenings and understand their rationale. It means adapting school and classroom practices when possible to fit the child's home culture. This helps parents feel heard, welcomed, and comfortable asking questions and voicing opinions.

A fundamental belief: Differences, not deficits

How we view families from cultures different than our own deeply affects how we work with them. Families from different cultures have had different sets of experiences. As teachers, we can best help students learn if we believe their family experiences are neither better nor worse than our own, but simply different.

Literacy professor Victoria Purcell-Gates wrote about this "difference" versus "deficit" view of family backgrounds after doing a two-year study of children from economically stressed homes. As school teachers know well, children come to school having had widely varying experiences with reading, writing, and other literacy activities at home, and even English speakers come speaking different dialects of English. But, Purcell-Gates points out, if the family is poor, is undereducated, or speaks a "nonstandard" dialect, we're more likely to interpret a child's uniqueness as some sort of inherent deficit or flaw in the child or parents rather than a mere difference in experience. When we do this, she says, we risk lowering our expectations of the child, writing the child off as less teachable or even unteachable. By contrast, when we truly believe that all children can learn and that they only vary in the kinds of experiences they've had, we're more likely to maintain high expectations of all the children and, in a nonjudgmental way, build on the experiences they *have* had to help them learn at their best in school. (Delpit and Dowdy 2002, 121–139)

The "difference" versus "deficit" view comes into play in areas beyond language and literacy as well. Bonnie Baer-Simahk, a teacher of K–6 English language learners in Massachusetts, tells of working with students from Southeast Asia. Early in her career, she was surprised to learn that many of these students didn't like to take their completed schoolwork home because their parents would throw it away. "I was so upset about this, thinking that the message the parents gave to the children was that their schoolwork was not valued," she recalls. "Later it became apparent that I was quite wrong in my interpretation." The same parents who never displayed their children's work on the refrigerator or on the wall welcomed Bonnie into their home to talk about their children's progress in school. They came to school to help out whenever invited. In their halting English they urged Bonnie to tell them if their children weren't doing good work in school. They also demonstrated their respect each day for their children's growing mastery of English, says Bonnie, by counting on the children to read their mail, to help them at the post office, and to serve as interpreters as they navigated life in their new country. Clearly, these parents valued their children's school efforts. There must have been another explanation for why they didn't display the children's schoolwork.

What was the explanation? "I suspect it was a combination of things," says Bonnie. Maybe the parents didn't understand the significance of the papers or the teacher's comments on them, she says. Maybe it was because they trusted the school system totally to do its job and believed that their own role was to stay out of the way. Maybe their expectation for their children to work hard was so deeply ingrained that positive efforts didn't require any special acknowledgment or celebration. Maybe not displaying the children's work stemmed from their cultural belief that children should be taught to be humble and self-effacing. Whatever the reason, the point is that the parents' behavior reflects a *difference* in experience and norms, not a lack of care or concern for their children.

Whether it's literacy experiences, keeping and displaying children's work, or some other issue, we can best teach children when we hold fast to the "difference, not deficit" mentality. When we do this, we're more likely to see intelligence, talent, caring, and kindness, even if these are expressed in ways that we're not used to. We can then build on these assets to teach the children what they need to learn in our classrooms.

Practical Strategies

Practical Strategies

Here are four strategies that can help us fully engage parents of different cultures:

- Learn about cultures other than our own whenever possible.

- Put ourselves in parents' shoes.

- Look to parents as a resource in solving problems.

- Bring families' cultures into the classroom curriculum.

Learn about cultures other than our own whenever possible

In order to teach students, we have to know them. One important way to know them is to connect with their families and communities, which means spending time learning about their cultures.

This learning is most rewarding and interesting when we can do it in depth. As bilingual teacher Lizette Román writes, "To have knowledge of another culture does not mean to be able to repeat one or two words in a student's language, nor is it to celebrate an activity or sing a song related to their culture. To acknowledge and respect is to be able to understand and apply this knowledge to everyday classroom activities. It is to be able to make changes or modifications in one's curriculum or pedagogy when the needs of the students have not been served." (Nieto 1999, 144)

So beyond repeating some words and singing some songs, what knowledge of families' cultures are we talking about?

Here are some of the areas to be aware of:

Nonverbal communication behaviors—the appropriate physical distance between speakers; what eye contact means; whether touching is appropriate; what kinds of body postures are considered respectful

Conversation norms—who should start a conversation; what it means to interrupt; how silences are used in conversation; how to bring up sensitive topics

Values related to children's learning—how adults teach children discipline, exercise their authority, and reinforce rules and values; whether cooperative or independent learning tends to be more valued; how adults support children in gaining independence

Cultural history—the culture's contributions to science, the arts, education, sports, and other fields; its folk heroes; its legends; its politics

As we learn about different cultures, it's essential to keep in mind that no one set of characteristics or values will be true of all members of a particular cultural group. It helps, therefore, to combine whatever descriptions we read or hear about a culture with our own knowledge of the individual families with whom we're working. Also, because much of what's written about minority groups reinforces existing stereotypes, it's important to look for information from a variety of sources. (See the box "Resources for Learning about Different Cultures" on page 16.)

Acquiring information about other cultures is the first important step; the next harder step is to get that information into our psyches so that we can change our ingrained habits when a situation demands it. Massachusetts teacher Bonnie Baer-Simahk tells of meeting the father of a student from Pakistan. As she approached, Mr. Khan smiled broadly and greeted her. Bonnie automatically held out her hand to shake his. He shook her hand, but visibly stiffened and

Practical Strategies

Resources for Learning about Different Cultures

The child and the parents themselves: This is one of the most important sources of help in understanding the family's culture. Try to inform parents honestly that you don't know a lot about their culture, and you want their help in learning about it. Most parents don't expect teachers to be experts on their culture and are happy to help if they feel respected.

Colleagues: Teachers of English language learners, home liaisons, other teachers, instructional assistants, and office or other staff may have knowledge of particular cultures and direct experience working with families of different backgrounds. Start conversations with them about the issues you're facing in working with parents. They may have ideas or skills to offer.

Your school as a whole: Ask to have conversations as a whole staff about cultural and language issues in working with parents. Staff at each grade level could learn about a particular issue over the course of the year and share the information with the rest of the school.

Other schools: Find out if there are other schools serving the same family populations as you do. See what they've tried.

Community organizations: Libraries, refugee organizations, churches, other religious organizations, civic groups, and local universities are all possible sources of help.

The Internet: The Internet contains a wealth of information and practical strategies for working with parents from diverse cultures. It also contains misinformation, so rely on credible sources. Here are a few sites to check out:

- Educator's Reference Desk℠: www.eduref.org/cgi-bin/res.cgi/Specific_Populations/Minority_Groups

- National Clearinghouse for English Language Acquisition & Language Instruction Educational Programs: www.ncela.gwu.edu

- Tolerance.org: www.tolerance.org

recoiled somewhat. Mr. Khan apologized, explaining that in his culture it was forbidden for a man to shake a woman's hand. "He told me he knew better, that it was different in America, but he was new and couldn't help his reaction," Bonnie recalls. Bonnie apologized too, immediately remembering what she'd learned about Pakistani culture and realizing her mistake in offering her hand. "But like Mr. Khan, I am a product of my upbringing and culture," says Bonnie. "My automatic handshake was as natural to me as it was unnatural to him. I had read articles about Pakistani culture, and Mr. Khan was well-read on U.S. culture. We both knew better. Our reaction had less to do with what we knew than who we were." Fortunately, Bonnie and Mr. Khan both saw the humor in the situation. They laughed about the awkward moment and went on with their conversation.

Bonnie's story is instructive. It reminds us to make that extra effort to go from knowing something to securing it in our consciousness so that our knowledge translates into behavior. Her story also reminds us that we all make mistakes even when we know better. Finally, the story tells us to forgive ourselves and others for making mistakes, to learn from the errors, to go forward with a positive attitude, and to keep trying.

Put ourselves in parents' shoes

To work well with parents from various cultures, it's important to put ourselves in their shoes and try to see the world as they see it. School can look and feel very different to different populations in the United States, and their relationships with school may differ dramatically as a result. There are parents who interact with teachers frequently and with ease. There are parents who advocate for services and programs for their child with tireless energy. And there are parents who, wary of the educational establishment, maintain a distant relationship with the teacher.

One kindergarten teacher tells of a student named Andre who nearly missed a field trip because his mother, a beginner at speaking English, misunderstood the departure time. The children had been told repeatedly that they were to arrive at school at 8:30 as usual, and that the bus for the field trip would pull away from the school at 9:30 sharp. Notes were sent home saying the same thing. It was expected that Andre would explain the situation to his mother. Something, however, got lost in the translation. On field trip day, the child and his mother didn't show up until the teacher was about to give up and tell the bus to go.

What was notable about the incident wasn't the fact that there was confusion about the arrival time, says the teacher, but the fact that the mother didn't ask the school for clarification. "It must've seemed odd to her, because this was late in the year, and school had started at 8:30 every day, even on days with special events," the teacher says. Moreover, the school had a home liaison who spoke the family's language. The mother could've talked to her. Still, the mother didn't call. "She was very receptive to whatever was offered to her, but she wouldn't come to the school or the teacher to ask questions herself," the teacher observes. "Even with a liaison in place, we still need to reach out actively to parents."

Practical Strategies

Many parents who don't proactively contact the school or teacher are those who feel like outsiders because of their race, ethnicity, economic status, educational background, proficiency with English, or immigrant status. Sara Lawrence-Lightfoot, education professor and author of the book *The Essential Conversation: What Parents and Teachers Can Learn from Each Other,* makes the following observation of many new immigrant families:

> Their reticence is born of not knowing the language, customs, or idioms of the new country; not knowing the norms, rules, and rituals of classrooms; and not feeling welcomed by a school bureaucracy that seems opaque and impenetrable. Not knowing all of these things makes them stay away from their child's classrooms and leaves their offspring to negotiate the school on their own. (Lawrence-Lightfoot 2003, 127–128)

As a teacher, I find it helpful to ask myself, "If my home culture were different from the dominant culture of this school, what would I need and want from my child's teacher and the school? What would help me feel oriented, informed, and welcomed?"

Here are some ideas:

Acknowledge every child's family culture

As Urssla Ogbenta, a parent from Nigeria, says, "Teachers should find out what country *every* kid comes from. When we do 'multiculturalism,' we often miss someone in the class. The teacher can't learn the language of every child, but every child's culture can be represented in some small way. Maybe the class can read a book or put up a picture about that culture, or show the flag of that country. That makes the children and families feel more valued."

Keep letters sent home simple and to the point

For parents who prefer oral communication, call on the phone instead of relying only on written information.

Find people at school or in the community who can translate

They can translate letters sent home, interpret at meetings with parents, or serve as liaisons with families.

Find out if there are local newspapers in the families' languages

Place notices and articles about school happenings in these.

Offer clarifications proactively when confusion might be possible

This is more effective than waiting for parents to ask questions. The story above of Andre and the nearly missed field trip is an example.

Label spaces in the classroom and school in families' home languages

Label spaces such as the main office, library, cafeteria, and restrooms. This could be an all-school or classroom project. Parents could also be invited to help.

Chapter One

Help parents understand expectations for student work

Minneapolis teacher Kirstin Keto knows that many of the Hmong parents with whom she works have had no formal schooling and may not know what's expected of children in school. To help them understand, she often takes time during parent conferences to show them samples of successful student work.

Adjust classroom activities when possible to respect families' values

Some parents told Minneapolis teacher Jeremy Nellis that they weren't comfortable with the usual Valentine's Day celebration centering on hearts, sweets, and romance. Jeremy quickly adjusted by having students write compliments to each other on slips of paper instead of exchanging the usual cards and candies.

Understand and work with extended school absences

Families often need to return to their home countries for extended periods because of family obligations. When kindergarten teacher Manjula Ganesh of Fairfax, Virginia, learned that a student would be missing several weeks of school because of a trip back to Lebanon, she gave the father a stack of books. She showed him how to help the child read them and practice literacy skills during the time away. In New London, Connecticut, second and third grade teacher Candy Bartsch assigned a child the task of keeping a journal on his extended family trip to India. When the child returned, his sharing of the journal sparked rich learning for the whole class.

I want to voice one caveat: As we actively welcome parents into the arena of school, it helps to remember that even if we take all of the steps listed above and more, some parents may not respond as we hope. Some of them may be working two or three jobs to make ends meet and may simply not have time for school activities. Other parents might need to take a while to feel sure that they're welcome at school. They may need us to reassure them again and again that we value their input.

Finally, in some cultures, it may be the norm for parents to take a hands-off approach and trust that the school will take care of children's education. Kathleen Fay, a Fairfax County, Virginia, teacher experienced in teaching English language learners, tells about a Vietnamese mother. At a conference with her, Fay encouraged the mother to tell what her son was like at home and what concerns she had about his education. "[The mother] said simply, 'Thank you for teaching my son,' and repeated it again when we said good-bye," Fay writes. "We need to remember that sometimes parents won't want to open up to us, and that is okay." (Fay and Whaley 2004, 193)

Look to parents as a resource in solving problems

Even with our best proactive efforts to make school effective for children of different cultures, problems will arise. When individual children are having trouble during the school year, the best people to go to for help are the adults in their home life. This is true for all families regardless of their cultural background. After all, these adults are the experts on the family's environment—its values, child raising practices, and expectations—and the family environment critically influences how the child learns.

In her book *Other People's Children,* Lisa Delpit, a scholar and champion of improved education for urban and African American students, tells of a teacher, a European American, who was working with six- to eight-year-olds on journal writing. One child in particular, an African American, was filling his journal with beautiful, intricate drawings but rarely wrote more than a few words on a page. The teacher talked to the child's mother about how the teachers were trying to encourage children to do the writing first, but that the boy liked to draw. He asked how the mother would handle this at home. The mother said, "In Black families we would just tell him write the words first." When the teacher went back and said that to the child, the boy suddenly began writing one- to two-page entries in his journal. (Delpit 1995, 180)

Encourage Families to Preserve Their Home Language

According to many researchers and teachers of English language learners, an important way for parents to help children learn English and do well in school is to speak with their children in their home language. "Parents often believe mistakenly that they can best help their child by speaking English, or trying to speak English, at home," says Bonnie Baer-Simahk, an experienced teacher of English language learners in Fitchburg, Massachusetts. However, there is research that says learning two languages not only does not confuse children, but proficiency in the home language actually helps children learn a second language. Researchers believe this is because children use the literacy skills they develop in one language to learn skills in a second one.

Preserving their home language can also help children communicate with their parents and stay connected to their home cultures, important for all children regardless of their ethnic backgrounds. "I see many parents who can't communicate with their children, often because the parents don't speak English fluently and the children haven't kept up their home language," says Bonnie.

By encouraging parents to speak and read to their children in their home language, teach the songs and legends from their cultural tradition, and promote literacy in the home language in other ways, teachers are helping parents to help their children learn.

For research on this topic, see the following:

Cummins, Jim. 1991. "Interdependence of first- and second-language proficiency in bilingual children." In *Language Processing in Bilingual Children,* ed. E. Bialystok, 70–89. Cambridge: Cambridge University Press.

Fitzgerald, J. 1995. "English-as-a-Second-Language Learners' Cognitive Reading Processes: A Review of Research in the United States." *Review of Educational Research* (65): 145–190.

Thomas, Wayne P., and Virginia P. Collier. 2002. *A National Study of School Effectiveness for Language Minority Students' Long-Term Academic Achievement.* Santa Cruz, CA: Center for Research on Education, Diversity and Excellence, University of California-Santa Cruz.

Chapter One

In addition to helping us solve the problems at hand, asking for advice from parents puts us in the mindset of working collaboratively to meet a challenge. It communicates to parents, "We know you know your child better than anyone else and we value what you have to say."

Bring families' cultures into the classroom curriculum

As our nation's school-age population becomes increasingly diverse, many teachers and schools are working harder at offering multicultural education. It's now common for classes to observe various cultures' holidays, eat their foods, and don their costumes, often during special times of year such as Black History Month or Chinese New Year.

Practical Strategies

But many in the field of multicultural education are suggesting that we go beyond studying other cultures' artifacts, holidays, and foods—an approach that a Los Angeles school board member called "one food, two heroes and three holidays" (Swap 1993, 39). Though fully well-intentioned, teachers taking this approach run the risk of including cultures in only a shallow way. In reflecting on my own past teaching, I see that I myself often included various cultures in this "add-on" way.

Instead, many educators say, the content of the curriculum itself needs to reflect more of the views, values, history, and learning styles of our students' families. And the main goal of this, to emphasize an earlier point, is to help students learn the concepts and skills they are supposed to learn in school.

It may seem overwhelming to integrate families' cultures into the curriculum, especially if there are a number of different cultures represented in the classroom. But there are manageable ways to do this.

Here are three examples:

Build projects and lessons around families' interests

Heath, Massachusetts, primary teacher Deborah Porter spends time getting to know parents and finding out about their hobbies, expertise, and family traditions. She then invites parents into the classroom to share these things with the children. One parent taught the class to weave. Another taught the children how to quilt. Others taught the children how to organize an agricultural fair. All these are part of the culture of the small rural town where the children live. Whatever a parent shares, Deborah uses it to teach concepts and skills in math, social studies, science, and other content areas. In this way, the culture of the children's home and community becomes central to, rather than added onto, their everyday school learning. (See page 110 for a detailed description.)

Build lessons around students' interests

Lisa Delpit describes her experience at a middle school that is ninety-eight percent African American. After seeing how obsessed the students were with grooming their hair, it dawned on her that teachers could build endless lessons around hair. In science, there could be studies about the chemical properties of the hair dressing that many of the students were carrying around in their backpacks. In social studies, the students could learn about hairstyles and their social significance throughout history in different cultures. They could interview braiders about the cultural significance of different braiding patterns. In math, they could use African braiding as a way to study patterns and tessellations. "The object is not to lower standards or just teach what is interesting to the students," writes Delpit, "but to find the students' interests and build an academic program around them." (Delpit and Dowdy 2002, 45)

Find out about students' cultural heritage and build it into the curriculum

Lisa Delpit tells about another teacher, Stephanie Terry, who teaches in a Baltimore, Maryland, school with a 100 percent African American enrollment. Terry reads and studies on her own to learn about her students' ancestral culture. Whatever subject she teaches, she then connects it to the students' heritage. In a unit about libraries, she tells them about some of the world's first libraries in Africa. In a unit on health, she teaches students about early African doctors who wrote some of the first texts on medicine. In broadening students' perspectives, she also teaches about the contributions of Asian Americans, Native Americans, and Hispanic Americans. "Stephanie does not replace the current curriculum; rather, she expands it," writes Delpit. Stephanie's students learn their school subjects and they "learn to love themselves, love their history, and love learning." (Delpit 1995, 181–182)

Giving Home Cultures a Central Place

Many parents feel that when their children go off to school, they must leave their home culture at the classroom door. But if we are to successfully educate all our students, we must open the door wide to these home cultures and give them a central place in our teaching. We would be able to teach better, students would be able to learn better, and parents would be more able to support their children's learning.

Spotlight:

Somali Folktale Project

All Grades
Lyndale Community School
Minneapolis, Minnesota

**Spotlight:
Somali
Folktale
Project**

From the moment the first wave of Somali refugees came to Minneapolis in the mid-1990s, the Somali parents were telling teachers at Lyndale Community School that they wanted to help their children succeed in school. "Tell me what to do," parents would say through a translator. "My English is not good, but give me math problems to do with my child."

"I was frustrated because these Somali parents were asking to help in their children's learning process, but we didn't have a good way to include them or to offer a curriculum that reflected their background and experiences," says Charmaine Owens, a teacher of English language learners at Lyndale, where about a quarter of the 300 students are from Somalia. The language barrier and the Somali families' unfamiliarity with U.S. culture, combined with the fact that not all of the Somali parents or their children had formal education growing up, made it difficult for teachers and the Somali parents to work together actively to support the children's education.

Then Charmaine happened on something. In studying up on Somali culture, she learned that the camel was a prized and beloved animal that was central to the Somali nomadic lifestyle. She asked the Somali students to share with the class their experiences with camels. For homework, the children were to ask their parents for three camel stories. But instead of three, most children came back with dozens of stories—folktales, personal stories, stories heard from a relative or friend. Charmaine knew she had hit on something.

Why not collect Somali folktales from the parents, write them up, and use them in the classroom curriculum? English translations of the stories could be used in all kinds of literacy lessons, and the stories could spawn lessons in geography, social studies, history, science, and more. The Somali children would have classroom content that was relevant to their home cultures, and the whole class would benefit from learning about a new culture. Best of all, the Somali parents, because they're familiar with the stories, would be able to help their children with schoolwork related to the stories without needing to know English.

Developing a packet of stories and supporting materials

The English Language Learning (ELL) team went into action. Muhamed Ahmed, Maryan Ali, and others on the team called many Somali families in the school, asking them to contribute one folktale—not just about camels, but also about hyenas, goats, sheep, foxes, animal herders, kings, and anything else that might figure in the stories they grew up with. If the parent could write the story in Somali, the Somali speakers on the team would translate it into English. If the parent couldn't write it in Somali, s/he could tell the story to the child, who would tell it to a bilingual staff member at school. The staff member would write the story down.

Out of many stories contributed, the ELL team chose nineteen that would be appropriate for use with children in school. They produced two written versions of each story—one in English and one in Somali. They sent the Somali versions to Ibrahim Ayan, a local scholar who was an expert in written Somali, to polish up the writing. Then Charmaine developed a series of suggested classroom activities to go with each story, including discussion and background research questions, fill-in-the-missing-word exercises, plot sequencing activities, and a play that students could act out.

These materials were then distributed to other teachers at the school. Although originally intended for use in K–3 classrooms, the materials soon became popular in classrooms all the way through sixth grade. Then the district got interested and printed all the folktales and supporting materials in booklet form to give to staff in professional development trainings.

A bridge between home and school

As the team hoped, the Somali folktales now serve as a bridge between home and school for the Somali families. When children come home repeating the stories they're learning in school, the parents can enrich them by offering plot variations or telling how they learned the stories themselves as children. When the children have homework related to the stories, the parents can help by clarifying the plot, helping interpret the moral of the story, or offering background information.

"The Somali parents love this project," says Charmaine. "When they arrived in this country, it must've been impressed upon them the necessity of education in order for their children to succeed. They came eager and enthusiastic to help their children. And here is a way they can help."

Retaining Somali culture

Besides helping the Somali children learn English and providing their parents an entry into the U.S. school system, the folktale project also has the express goal of helping the children retain their Somali culture. Because of the long years of war in Somalia, many of the students have spent much or all of their lives in refugee camps and on the move, with little contact with their extended families or their native land. "These children have not had the opportunity to be immersed in their own culture," says Charmaine. By making Somali folktales a focal point of their school studies, the ELL team aims to encourage the children to learn about and value their cultural roots.

Spotlight: Somali Folktale Project

Writing down the stories in both English and Somali, for example, was a conscious move to promote literacy in both languages. In addition, Muhamed Ahmed, a Somali member of the ELL team, sometimes comes into the classrooms to tell the stories. With the children gathered at his feet, he tells the stories as his grandmother told them to him and as her grandfather told them to her. "Somalis have a rich oral tradition, and oral storytelling is one way they communicated their values," says Charmaine. When the children experience hearing a story from a Somali elder, they gain an appreciation of this traditional form of communication, she explains.

And of course it's not just the Somali children who gain an appreciation of Somali culture. All the school's children and staff have learned from the stories. "These parents are not only helping their own children, but they're helping others in the building to develop an appreciation for their new friends from Somalia," says Charmaine.

Story 1
The Hyena and the Fox

Once upon a time a fox became a problem to a nomadic settlement. This fox attacked and ate their goats and sheep. One day the people gathered together to plan how they could kill this troublesome fox. The people decided to set a trap.

The fox fell into the trap that was set for her. After awhile, the people came and tied her to a tree. The peop̶ ̶ ̶ ̶ ̶ ̶ to throw the fox into the fire.

They dug a hole near the tree wher̶ ̶ ̶ ̶ ̶ ̶ gathered wood and they put the wood int̶ ̶ ̶ ̶ ̶ said, "Let's come back when the fire is̶ ̶ ̶ ̶ troublesome fox into the hole."

Soon after the people left, a ver̶ ̶ ̶ the fox whining. He came closer, think̶ ̶ ̶ was very surprised to see that the̶ ̶ ̶ happened?" he asked.

The fox answered, "My uncle̶ ̶ ̶ ̶ He tied me to this tree because h̶ ̶ ̶ out to kill a goat to cook in this̶ ̶ ̶ am not hungry now because I've̶ ̶ ̶ time I try to escape, my uncle ̶ ̶ ̶ me eat more meat. Every time̶ ̶ ̶ my uncle will kill me if I can't̶ ̶ ̶

The hyena opened her̶ ̶ ̶ her favorite food. The fox̶ ̶ ̶ tie you up. Then you can e̶ ̶ ̶ The hyena agreed to the̶ ̶ ̶ hyena to the tree.

When the people̶ ̶ ̶ tree, they found the h̶ ̶ ̶ and said, "Hyena, whe̶ ̶ ̶

Story 1
SHEEKADA KOWAAD
WARAABE IYO DAWACO

Bari ayaa dawaco adhi fara badan ka cuni jirtay reero meel deggan. Adhigaas oo riyo iyo idaba lahaa. Maalin danbe ayaa dadkii meel isugu yimaadeen wax-aaney ka wada hadleen sidii ay dawacadaa dhibta badan iskaga dili lahaayeen. Waxay dadkii talo ku gaadheen in dabin loo dhigo dawacada. Dawacadii waxay ku dhacday dabinkii loo dhigay. Dadkii waxay ku xidheen dawacadii geed jiridiis, si looga aarsado oo waxaa talo lagu gaadhey in dab lagu dhex rido.

Dadkii waxay soo gureen qoryo xaabo ah oo aad u badan. Waxay xaabadii ka buuxsheen god aad u weyn oo ay ka qodeen geedkii ay dawa-cadu ku xidhnayd agtiisa. Markaas ayey xaabadii dab ku huriyeen waxayna yidhaahdeen, "Aan iska tagno, oo marka dabku uu aad u shidmo ku soo noqonno oo dawacada ku dhex ridno." Waraabe aad u gaajaysan ayaa wuxuu maqlay cidii dawacada. Markaas ayuu soo orday oo is yidhi, aad ka eryatid neefka ay dilootey maanta, waraabihii wuxuu u yimi dawacadii xidhneyd.

Intuu yaabey ayuu ku yidhi, "Naa dawaco yaa geedka kugu xidh-xid-hay?" Markaas ayey dawacadii tidhi, "Waxa igu xidhay adeerkay." Waraabihii (Dhurwaa) ayaa hadana yidhi, "Oo muxuu kuu xidhay?" Dawacadii ayaa tidhi, "Adeerkay aad buu ii jicelyahay." Wuxuu arkay in aan caato ahay markaa wuxuu ii qalay wan weyn oo aad u buuran. Dabkaasna wankaas ayaa lagu karin doonaa. Aniguna waan diidanahay in aan cuno wankaas buuran, waayo gaajo ima hayso oo maalmahan oo dhan ayaan hilib cunayey, oo wax-aan ka cabsanayaa inaan calool xanuun ka qaado. Markii aan damcay in aan ka tagana, intuu i soo qabtay ayuu geedkan igu xidhay. Markaan hilibkii cuni kari waayeyna wuu i diley.

Waraabihii ayaa intuu afka aad u kala qabtay illeen waa wax hilib iyo baruur jecele yidhi, "Ihi! ihi! ihi! aniga ayaa xariga kaa furaya ee aniga geedka igu xidh, si aan anigu u cuno hilibkaas adiguna uga nabad gasho." Markii dadkii ku soo noqdeen meeshii dawacadu ku xidhnayd, si ay dabka ugu dhex tuuraan, waxay u yimaaddeen waraabe ku xidhan geedkii. Dadkii ayaa intey yaabeen yidhi, "War Waraabe meeday dawacadii?" Markaas ayuu waraabihii yidhi, "aniga ayaa xarigii ka furay oo way tagtay."

Chapter One

The Somali folktales from parents were written down in English and Somali, a conscious move to promote students' literacy in both languages.

**Spotlight:
Somali
Folktale
Project**

Story 1
The Hyena and the Fox
A Play

Time: A long time ago
Place: In the country in Somalia where sheep and goats graze
Characters: narrator   herdsman 1
             fox   herdsman 2
             hyena   herdsman

Narrator: A long time ago a fox attacke[d]
             of some Somali herdsmen. T[he]
             fox. The fox was caught a[nd]
             Let me go! Let me go!
Fox:
Herdsman 1: Let's dig a hole next to t[he]
             wood for a fire.
Herdsman 2: Great idea! We can th[row]
             some fox.
Herdsman 3: This fox will never b[e]
Fox: Wait, don't burn me[]
             eat your sheep an[d]
Herdsman 1: Ha, ha.
Herdsman 2: Sorry, fox. We'l[l]
Herdsman 3: You have killed[]
             your turn to di[e]
             (Makes whinin[g]
Fox: While the h[]
Narrator: hyena heard[]
             that the f[ox]
Hyena: Maybe I[]
             that? Fo[]
Fox: Oh! My[]
             I am s[]
             sheep[]

Story 1
The Hyena and the Fox
Cloz activity

Fill in the missing words in the story using the following words:

ache	found	makes	threw
answered	found	meal	throw
because	fox	meat	tie
brought	goats	mouth	trap
cook	gone	nomadic	tree
decided	hole	people	uncle
died	hungry	plan	untie
escape	hungry	returned	untie
favorite	hyena	set	whining
favorite	instead	steal	wood
fire	kill	stomach	

Once upon a time a fox became a problem to a _____ settlement.
This fox attacked and ate their _____ and sheep. One day the peo-
ple gathered together to plan how they could kill this troublesome fox.
The people decided to set a _____.
    The fox fell into the trap that was _____ for her. After
awhile, the _____ came and tied her to a tree. The people
_____ to throw the fox into the _____. The people
They dug a hole near the _____ where the fox was tied, and
they gathered _____ and they put the wood into the _____.
They lit a fire, and said, "Let's come back when the _____ is ready.
Then we will _____ this troublesome fox into the hole."
    Soon after the people left, a very _____ hyena came by. He
heard the fox _____. He came closer, thinking he could
_____ the fox's _____. He was very surprised to see that
the fox was tied up to a _____. "What happened?" he asked.
    The fox _____, "My _____ tied me here. My uncle
really loves me. He tied me to this tree _____ he saw how thin and

*Each folktale had a set of accompanying classroom activities
that reinforced literacy and other skills.*

Spotlight:

Little Things That Make a Big Difference

All Grades
Regional Multicultural Magnet School
New London, Connecticut

When it comes to helping parents of different cultures feel comfortable around school, everyday efforts make a big difference, say teachers at Regional Multicultural Magnet School in New London, Connecticut. This K–5 school emphasizes a multicultural curriculum, offering, for example, Spanish language instruction for all students. The school has a sizeable Spanish-speaking population and offers a two-way bilingual program that allows all Spanish-speaking students who so choose to be in classrooms where the instruction is given in both English and Spanish. Others students are also invited to join the bilingual program and are selected for the limited slots through a lottery system.

Chapter One

In addition, the school has made the full inclusion of Spanish-speaking parents a part of its everyday culture through efforts such as the following:

Bilingual phone system

The tone of welcome and inclusion is established the first time a parent calls the school, and it's reinforced with every subsequent phone call. "Thank you for calling the Regional Multicultural Magnet School. For English, press 3," callers hear, and then immediately, "Gracias por llamar a la Escuela Multicultural. Para Español, oprima el 4." Spanish speakers can follow Spanish prompts to access the entire phone system.

Translating all written materials sent home

Newsletters, field trip reminders, and other notices and flyers sent home are written in both English and Spanish. Even report cards are translated for Spanish-speaking families. Such extensive translating is possible because the school has a number of bilingual office and teaching staff, including an office staff member whose job specifically includes translating. Primary teacher Margaret Sullivan says having the written materials in both languages "shows that we respect Spanish-speaking families. It speaks tons and sets up a good relationship." She adds, "It sends a message to non-Spanish speakers, too, that we value diversity."

Interpreters at family meetings

Whenever needed, bilingual staff members serve as interpreters at conferences and other meetings with parents. As with translating written materials, there is an established culture in which staff are willing to serve as interpreters if they possibly can, says principal Richard Spindler-Virgin.

Welcoming extended family to meetings

Recognizing the important role in child raising that grandparents, uncles, and aunts often have in Spanish-speaking families, the school makes it clear that extended family members are welcome to meetings, says Richard. Often, if a teacher knows that an adult other than the mother or father is the key decision maker or caregiver in the family, the teacher will specifically encourage that person to come.

**Spotlight:
Little Things
That Make a
Big Difference**

Meeting at off-site locations

If parents don't have transportation or prefer not to come to school, teachers offer to hold conferences and other meetings at alternative places: the local library, a coffee shop, a sandwich place, or the families' home. Some parents may be uncomfortable at school because school represents "authority" or because they think it's not their "place" to tell teachers what they think and feel about their children's education, says Richard. Meeting the teacher in a neutral public place or in their own homes can put them more at ease, he says.

Studying, not celebrating, holidays

Rather than celebrating Kwanzaa, Christmas, Thanksgiving, Valentine's Day, and other holidays, the children study them as part of social studies. For example, they might learn about the history of Valentine's Day, but they don't send cards or candy to each other. Teachers also invite parents to share holidays from their own cultures so that the children can study them. The teachers try to be sensitive to any parent concerns around holidays. Second and third grade teacher Candy Bartsch, for example, talks with parents about these studies during goal-setting conferences at the beginning of the year. Just before beginning an exploration of any holiday, she again contacts parents to let them know what will be coming up. If any parent feels any hesitation or discomfort with their child learning about certain holidays, Candy talks with the parent to try to understand their perspective.

Summing up the school's efforts to create an inclusive environment for families of all cultures, Margaret, the primary teacher, says, "We really just try to respect parents in little ways. It can be a little more work, but it's worth it."

**Chapter
One**

Chapter Two

P*arents don't always want to be on the receiving end of information. They want to feel valued and have a way to express their opinions. They want to feel that saying what's on their mind matters. Teachers can help them feel that way.*

Parent of a third grader

Actively investing in the first six weeks of school is just as important when working with parents as it is when working with children. In these early weeks, many teachers take specific steps to lay the groundwork for a successful year with their students, deliberately building a safe and welcoming classroom community. These teachers know that this is an investment that can make the whole school year go better. The same idea applies when working with parents: Investing in the first six weeks of school with parents can make interactions with them go better all year long.

This was not something I paid attention to when I first started teaching. I focused all my time and energy on the children and the happenings inside the four walls of my classroom. I had the children do activities to learn each other's names and get to know each other. I carefully established a classroom signal for quiet. I helped children think about and articulate their hopes and dreams for the year. I worked with the children to create classroom rules. I modeled and helped children practice what it meant to live by these rules. What I didn't do was pay attention to the people who resided outside the classroom walls, but who had a huge effect on classroom life: the families of my students.

It's not that I ignored parents completely. I sent out the routine letter introducing myself as their child's teacher and saying I looked forward to meeting all of them at open house and back-to-school night. I did one or two other perfunctory activities required of all teachers. But none of these things allowed me to connect with individual families at any deep level. Unless some problem arose with a particular child, the first time I had meaningful one-on-one time with parents was the first conference at the end of November. For the first three months of the school year, I was really keeping parents at a distance.

Looking back, I realize that I didn't know what else to do. I was a new teacher trying to keep my head above water. In addition, I didn't have a single course in college that offered practical strategies for truly engaging with my students' families.

Over the years, through learning from colleagues, through my own trial and error, and through talking and listening to parents, I discovered what experienced teachers know and what research has shown—that parent involvement is a leading component of a child's school success. I learned that children from all backgrounds are happier, more motivated, and get better grades when their parents take an active role in their education. I came to realize that investing in the first six weeks of school meant devoting time and energy to my students *and* their families.

Goals of Investing in the First Six Weeks

What does it mean to engage with parents in the first six weeks? What are the goals? To answer this question, we need only think about the goals of activities in the classroom during the first six weeks. One of the main goals there is to create a climate of warmth and safety by building trusting relationships among the teacher and students. There's a parallel with parents: Investing in parents during the first six weeks means creating a relationship of respect, trust, and collaboration with them.

Specifically, these are the main goals:

To help parents feel welcomed and valued

Parents should feel that the teacher is excited to have their child as a student and is looking forward to working with them throughout the year. They should feel secure that their opinions, concerns, interests, and family culture are important to the teacher.

To welcome parents to take an active role in their child's education

The first six weeks is the time to begin sending the message that parents are welcome to come to the classroom, send notes to the teacher, make phone calls, and voice opinions.

To help build a sense of community among families

The first six weeks is also the time to begin helping parents get to know each other. When parents have positive relationships among themselves, they're more likely to get their children together outside of school, take part in the life of the school, and seek help for their child when it's needed. All these help the child do better in school.

One parent of a second grader said, "It's so important to me that the teacher has a welcoming demeanor and warmth and openness, and shows that she's excited to have your child in the class and wants you to be a part of your child's education."

To have this type of relationship with parents, we need to set aside time to get to know them individually, acknowledge them as the expert on their child, and invite them into the educational partnership—and we need to start as early in the year as possible.

August or September: The First Parent Conference

A powerful way to show parents that they matter is to hold the first parent conference before school starts or during the early weeks of school, rather than waiting until November. This also allows the teacher to have crucial information about the child and the family early, which can mean more effective teaching of the child right from the very beginning of the year.

"Who is this child?": Listening to parents

Teachers may have expertise on child development, on specific teaching practices, and on the curriculum. But parents have the answers to the most important question when it comes to a child's learning: "Who is this child?"

We can teach a child so much more effectively when we have a true understanding of who the child is socially, emotionally, and intellectually. What is this child good at? What does she like to play? *How* does she like to play? What's hard for this child? How does he cope with frustration? Parents can provide a wealth of information in these areas that teachers might take months to learn or possibly never discover.

In *The Essential Conversation: What Parents and Teachers Can Learn From Each Other,* education professor Sara Lawrence-Lightfoot writes about Molly Rose, a first grade teacher in a school with a largely poor, newly immigrant population. During the first weeks of school, Molly sets up conferences with all her students' parents. She labels this first meeting a "listening conference," one in which the parent is the expert, and the teacher is seeking the parent's wisdom and guidance. To open the conversation, Molly asks a question that allows parents to say something that they're proud of in their child. "What is your child good at?" she might ask. "He's good at making friends," "She's a terrific soccer player," or even "She's good at setting the table," parents answer.

To ensure a 100 percent turnout at these conferences, Molly makes herself available any time of the day, before or after school. "We work through all kinds of scheduling complications," she says. "When [parents] break an appointment or do not show, I have no problem with that. I don't take it personally," she says. "We work until we can find another time." Her unyielding determination to meet the parents, along with her care in listening to them rather than talking at them, begins to establish a solid teacher-family relationship. (Lawrence-Lightfoot 2003, 62–64)

Inviting parents to share their goals

Another way to open the dialogue with parents is to ask, "What do you think is most important for your child to learn this year?" or "What's your biggest hope for your child this year?" Not only do these questions immediately engage the parent in a meaningful way, but they set a tone of collaboration, and the answers give teachers important insights into their new students.

It's a good idea to send a letter home beforehand to give parents time to think about their goals for their child. On the opposite page is an example from Boston, Massachusetts, teacher Gail Zimmerman.

Often it's difficult for parents to choose just one goal for their child. Allowing them to choose both an academic goal and a social goal, as Gail does in her letter, can take the pressure off. It also communicates the belief that the social curriculum is as important as the academic one.

Some social goals that parents have shared for their children are:

- "I wish she had more friends."

- "I want him to enjoy school more."

- "I want her to be better behaved."

- "I want him to do a better job following the teacher's directions."

Some academic goals that parents have shared are:

- "I want her to be a better speller."

August 14, 2004

Dear Parents:

Our first parent-teacher conferences will be held before school starts during the week of August 28th. This conference is a chance for teachers and parents to meet each other and begin building positive communications so that we can all better support your child's learning.

At this first meeting I will be asking you to share your hopes and dreams for your child this year. I'm really interested in what you think is most important for your child to learn. Please find an academic goal and a social goal which we can focus on together. I will be paying careful attention to these goals and keeping you informed of your child's progress throughout the year. At our conference I will also be sharing with you my goals for the class, in both the academic and social learning areas.

During the first week of school, your child will also be asked what s/he wants most to learn in school. All the children will share these hopes and dreams with the class. Then the class will create classroom rules that will allow all class members to achieve their goals.

In the middle of the year, we will evaluate your child's growth and decide whether to continue with the goals you and your child chose, or to choose new goals.

I look forward to meeting with you and working together to make this a safe, challenging, and joyful year for your child.

Sincerely,

Gail Zimmerman

Chapter Two

- "I wish he would read more and enjoy it."

- "I want him to learn his math facts."

- "I want her to read about and learn more history."

While parents generally choose goals that are appropriate for their child's grade and developmental stage, occasionally a parent will name a goal that is overly ambitious or inappropriate in some other way. For example, "I want him to write stories with correct spelling," a parent of a kindergartner might say. I've found that in these situations, it's best to probe further to find out what's behind the parent's wish. By listening carefully, I might learn that what the parent really wants is for the child to like writing and to care about doing quality work. I can then reassure the parent by saying, "The children will be doing lots of beginning writing activities this year. They'll be telling and recording stories, and I'll be working with them to grasp the concept of letters and spelling. My goal is to help them develop an appreciation for writing and for doing good work." As teacher Ruth Sidney Charney says about these discussions with parents, "The aim is not to contest or argue, but to understand and communicate." (Charney 2002, 127)

August or September: The First Parent Conference

Documenting parents' goals and children's progress

Whether it's a listening conference or a hopes-and-dreams conference, it's important that the teacher takes careful notes and keeps the documentation. Not only are written records an important reference for the teacher, but they send a message to parents that the teacher has heard and cares about what they think. In addition, if the discussion is about a parent's goal, it's important that the teacher tells the parent how the child's progress will be documented.

Parents may change their goal for their child as the year goes on. At the next parent conference, teachers might ask, "How do you think your child is doing in meeting the goal that you set?" and "Has your goal for your child changed?"

(For more about beginning-of-the-year parent conferences, see "Setting Out the Welcome Mat" on page 48.)

Family Interest Inventory

Another way to reach out to parents at the beginning of the year is to send out a family interest inventory. The form asks parents to list any special talents, skills, interests, or family traditions that they would be willing to share with the class. Not only does this establish a connection with the family, but it's an effective way to welcome parents to take an active role in the life of the classroom.

Here's a sample inventory form:

[Date]

Dear Parents,

Welcome to what I know will be a fulfilling and fun year of learning. Please briefly help me get to know your family.

What are some of your family's special interests (such as hobbies, skills, or the kind of work you do)? _____

_____

_____

_____

Would you be willing to come share your special interests with the children? _____

Additional information, special concerns, or questions for me:

_____

_____

_____

_____

Sincerely,

[Teacher's name]

Chapter Two

Once I've collected the inventories from parents, I make a list of all the things they are willing to share with the class. Rafael's mom is willing to show the class her coin collection. Marlene's dad can teach hand drumming. Anna's grandfather is willing to tell stories. As I plan units of study, I check the list and incorporate parents when possible. My goal is to include at some point during the year every parent who recorded something on the inventory. This offers a way for the whole class to learn about each other's families, to help the children and their parents feel welcome, and to bring rich resources into the curriculum. (For more on this topic, see "Building Families' Interests into the Curriculum" on page 110.)

A Sense of Community among Families

A Sense of Community among Families

At the same time that we're building a positive relationship with parents, we can be helping parents build positive relationships with each other. It's easier for parents to support their child's education when they have connections with other parents: They can have someone to call upon to pick up their child if they get stuck at work, someone to call to talk about a school assignment, someone to go to school events with, someone whose child can do homework with their child.

Teachers can encourage relationships among parents in various ways. Some of these are touched upon in later chapters of this book. Here, I'd like to highlight one method that I use, one involving a modified version of Morning Meeting.

(Other ideas in the book are the use of group email in Chapter 4, creating a parent publishing group in Chapter 5, and inviting parents to family literacy nights in Chapter 6.)

Morning Meeting at back-to-school night

I've found back-to-school night to be a good time to start helping parents form relationships with each other. When I plan a back-to-school night, I have several goals. I want to continue to get to know the students' parents, and I'd like them to continue to get to know me. I want to share with them my goals and expectations for the year. And I'd like to help parents get to know one another.

With these goals in mind, I begin the evening with a modified Morning Meeting. A component of the *Responsive Classroom*® approach to teaching and learning, Morning Meeting is a fifteen- to twenty-minute routine that takes place first thing in the classroom every day. Students and the teacher gather in a circle to greet one another, share and respond to each other's news, do a fun group activity that reinforces the skills the children are working on, and look forward together to the day ahead. Morning Meeting is a key feature in my classroom. It builds community, creates a climate of respect and trust, helps improve children's reading, writing, math, listening, and speaking skills—and the children love it. (For more on Morning Meeting, see *The Morning Meeting Book* by Roxann Kriete, published by Northeast Foundation for Children, 2002.)

Using a Morning Meeting format in the parent meeting is a natural choice. Just as the format sets a positive tone for learning in the classroom, it sets a positive tone for this evening of adult communication and collaboration. It helps build a sense of community among all of us adults, and it lets parents experience something their children do every day at school.

Although the content of these meetings is geared for adults, I stick to the usual Morning Meeting format as much as possible. As parents arrive, I stand at the classroom door, greeting and welcoming each one of them. I ask parents to take a look around the room, read the message that I wrote to them on the easel chart, and find a seat in the circle. When it's time to start the evening, I, too, sit in the circle with them.

Chapter Two

There's a specific reason for the circle seating. Typically, at back-to-school nights, the teacher is standing at the front of the room lecturing while the parents are sitting in rows or standing. Those standing in the back of the room are often straining to hear. The unintentional, or perhaps intentional, message is that the teacher is the caller of the shots, the most important person in the room.

Having everyone sitting in a circle, by contrast, emphasizes a feeling of collaboration and openness. I am no longer controller, but facilitator, of the evening's conversation and of the parents' involvement in their children's education for the year. The circle seating—and the entire Morning Meeting format and structure—also encourage parents to interact and get to know one another.

Incidentally, I use all adult-sized chairs for the meeting. Parents can wonder what the point is, not to mention be downright uncomfortable, when asked to sit in tiny child-sized chairs, especially if the teacher is sitting in a large, comfortable teacher chair.

Once the majority of the parents have arrived, we begin. We go through all four components of Morning Meeting just as the children do in class. Here's what the adult meeting might look like:

Greeting

We might do the "Interview Greeting." We each pair up with someone we don't know very well and interview that person to find out his/her name, child's name, and relationship to the child (parent, aunt, grandparent, etc.). We find out one thing our partner likes to do with the child. Then, going around the circle, we introduce our partners and tell the group what we learned about them.

Sharing

Whole-group sharing often works well. We all think of one thing we enjoy doing besides activities with our child. Going around the circle, each person shares this favorite activity in one to three words. Anyone who wants to pass is free to do so.

A Sense of Community among Families

Group Activity

An activity that I've had success with is "Table for…," in which I play a restaurant host calling for different numbers of people to be at a "table" together. When I say "Table for three!" parents put themselves into groups of three. (They don't really sit at a table; they just stand in a group.) Then I give a topic for a quick conversation—for example, "Tell each other where you grew up," "Tell your child's name and one thing your child likes to do," or "Name something you like to do as a family." Groups have about one minute to talk about whatever topic is named, then I ring a chime and say, "Table for four!" Parents get into a new group of four to talk about a new topic I give them. We continue like this for several more rounds.

Morning Message

Throughout Greeting, Sharing, and Group Activity, there's usually a lot of smiling, laughing, nodding—a lot of connections being made. By the time everyone returns to a seat after the activity, there's a different atmosphere in the room. Everyone seems to feel more relaxed, more welcomed, more like a community. We can now turn more productively to the business of the evening: the goals, classroom practices, and curriculum of their child's year ahead.

To make the transition, I bring out the message I've written on easel chart paper ahead of time, just as I would in class with the children:

Welcome, Fourth Grade Parents!

I'm so glad you're here with us tonight. I look forward to getting to know each of you more and having all of you get to know one another better. I look forward to sharing with you what life is like in our classroom and what you can expect in the year ahead.

Before we begin as a whole group at 7:15 PM, please:

- Take a look at your child's work hanging around the room.

- Take a look at our Hopes and Dreams display at the back of the room.

- Think of any questions you might have for me. If you wish, write one question you most want answered in the space below.

- Find a seat in the circle.

I'm looking forward to working with each of you this year.

Sincerely,

Carol Davis

Chapter Two

After reading the message together, we move into the rest of the evening, making the segue by reading aloud the questions that parents jotted down on the chart. In my presentation, I explain the discipline approach I'll be using and give an overview of the curriculum, being sure to answer the questions that parents wrote on the chart as I go along. I invite questions and comments often.

At the end of the evening, I always notice parents seeking one another out, talking about their children or commenting on the evening. The ice has been broken and parents are taking the first steps to form relationships.

Guidelines for Leading a Morning Meeting with Parents

Some adults feel right at home in a school setting. Others may feel awkward and unsure of what to do. Some may feel they have already taken a big risk just coming to school. Here are some things that can help the meeting go better for everyone:

Greet parents individually at the door when they arrive

Be sure to make this one-on-one contact with every parent.

Provide name tags

This helps parents learn each other's names and become comfortable using them.

Introduce the meeting

A short introduction is all that's needed. For example, you might say, "Morning Meeting is a fifteen- to twenty-minute routine that our class begins every day with. It helps build a sense of community, sets a positive tone for the day, and improves academic and social skills. You'll now have a chance to experience a version of this meeting first-hand."

Choose low-risk activities that help parents get to know each other

Especially at the beginning of the year, avoid greetings and activities that are too silly or that require physical contact. Avoid activities that could embarrass anyone.

Keep any sharings brief and focused

Going around the circle to share on a common, simple topic is often effective because it lets everyone say something (or pass) but does not require questions and comments.

Use the message chart to launch into the discussion of the curriculum

For example, the message might ask parents to write one question they have about the curriculum. Reading the questions together is a way to segue into the discussion.

A Sense of Community among Families

Take a few minutes to reflect together on the meeting

Before launching into the discussion following the meeting, have the group talk about how they feel now compared to when they first entered the room, and what social and academic skills were practiced in the meeting. This can help them see the benefits of Morning Meeting for their children.

Follow up with written information about Morning Meeting

Periodically talk about Morning Meeting in letters and class newsletters sent home. For those who could not attend the meeting, this is valuable information. For those who were present, it's a good reminder of what they learned and experienced during the meeting.

(To learn more about using the Morning Meeting format with adults, see Appendix A.)

Chapter Two

A Common Understanding about Homework

The first six weeks of school is also the time for teachers to communicate carefully with parents about their homework approach. Homework is something that teachers, parents, and students all have strong feelings about. Many teachers are frustrated with students not doing homework. Parents are often surprised by the amount or difficulty of the work teachers give, or they're tired of having to nag their children into getting the work done. Students are too often just plain sick of homework.

Thinking back on my early teaching years, I remember resenting parents for not helping children get their homework done. I kept asking, "Why can't parents help me out in this one area?"

As I got to know the different parents I was working with, I was able to come up with some good answers to this question. Most of my students came from single-parent or two-worker families. By the time everyone got home and had dinner, there was little time for the adults to help with homework if they wanted to get the children to bed at a decent hour. In addition, some parents lacked the skills, the language, or the understanding of current educational approaches to help their children with the assignments I was giving. Some parents didn't know how to help their children manage time and take responsibility to complete the homework on their own.

Once I had this picture, I realized I needed to make some changes. Knowing that many parents are unable to help their children with homework, I began assigning only work that children could do independently, which meant work that had them practicing a skill they already learned in school. Realizing how busy many families' evenings are, I decided that assignments should not be too lengthy or time-consuming.

These changes went along well with my developing beliefs about homework, which were that it should support, rather than add to, what was covered in class, and that it should never be a burden for the students or their families.

Schools and teachers will vary in their beliefs about the purpose of homework and what the appropriate amount is. Regardless of these variations, the important thing is to consider parents' concerns and communicate homework policies and practices to them clearly.

The Small
Daily
Interactions
That Matter
So Much

At K.T. Murphy School in Stamford, Connecticut, for example, an information packet about the school-wide homework policy is sent home to parents in early September. The packet includes a letter explaining the homework policy and procedures, a checklist of homework expectations, and tips to help parents set up a work area and a designated time for their children to do homework.

Many teachers, knowing they cannot assume that children know how to do homework, spend the first weeks of school actively teaching children these skills. All "homework" assignments are done during school time with considerable teacher guidance at first, and less as time goes on. Only when the children can demonstrate that they know how to do this "homework" independently do teachers begin giving assignments that are truly to be done at home.

Once homework gets under way, careful communication with parents remains crucial. Many teachers send home weekly or daily homework sheets that let parents know what's expected of their child that day or week.

(For more about this topic, see "Healthy Homework" on page 51.)

The Small Daily Interactions That Matter So Much

Parents' hopes and dreams, the first parent conference, back-to-school night, homework. These are the big things that we need to handle with care and skill when building bridges with parents at the start of the school year. But as we go about these early weeks, it's important not to forget the small daily interactions that also matter so much.

Whenever a parent drops off or picks up a child, calls to get the homework assignment for a sick child, or comes to help out in the classroom, that's a golden opportunity to make a connection in a meaningful, if small, way: We can follow up on something previously discussed, mention a positive thing the child did at school, or simply ask how the parent is doing. These small, daily encounters let parents know that we recognize and value them.

Reaching Out as Early as Possible

The partnership of school and home can be one of our most powerful unions. Building this union begins with reaching out and engaging parents as early in the school year as possible. There are a variety of ways to do this—the methods described in this chapter are suggestions and guidelines. Each of us will want to figure out what works best for us and for the parents of our particular class. The important things are that we are informative, respectful, and welcoming, and that we begin early.

Chapter Two

Spotlight:

Setting Out the Welcome Mat: The First Parent Conference

Third Grade
Rolling Hills Elementary School
Holland, Pennsylvania

Like many schools, Rolling Hills Elementary in Holland, Pennsylvania, holds its first parent conferences as a school in November. But that hasn't kept third grade teacher Susan Smith from meeting and talking with her students' parents as early as the first days of school.

Before school starts in August, Susan sends a letter to each parent, inviting the parent to come for a ten- to fifteen-minute meeting with her before or after school sometime during the first weeks. She explains that the purpose of the meeting is for them to tell her their hopes and dreams for their child for the year. To facilitate the conversation, she asks parents to jot down their hopes and dreams on a simple form and to bring the form to the meeting. (See sample on page 49.)

One parent said he wanted his child to become a more confident reader. Another wanted her child to be a leader sometimes, not always a follower. A third parent wanted her child to learn the multiplication tables.

"Basically, I'm listening," Susan says of her role in these early meetings. "I'm getting an important first glimpse at each family's priorities."

The fact that these meetings take place very early in the year is crucial. "Parents usually don't get to talk to their child's teacher until months into the school year, unless something goes wrong or unless they call and set up an appointment," says Susan. When the teacher makes the first move early to invite parents to share what they think is important for their child, a tone of interest, respect, and collaboration is set right from the beginning. "I like to think a partnership is being developed," Susan says.

Beyond asking parents about their hopes and dreams, Susan also invites them to share any information that might help her be a more effective teacher for the child. Parents are generally forthcoming about a special strength, challenge, or personality trait in their children that might affect their learning. One parent told Susan that her child tended to be a perfectionist and gets extremely frustrated if

---

Hopes and Dreams

Child's name: <u>Nicholas</u>

Parent's name: <u>Paula</u>

My hopes and dreams for my child's academic learning this year are:

I would like Nicholas to learn to write neater, to take his time with directions and not try to rush his way through school. I would also like for Nicholas to enjoy learning and being in school.

My hopes and dreams for my child's social development this year are:

I want Nicholas to build strong friendships. I want him to learn that he can resist peer pressure and still be liked. I would like him to be more assertive in approaching people and in speaking his mind.

Chapter Two

---

she doesn't understand something or doesn't do well on an assignment. Hearing this alerted Susan to watch for that tendency in the child, and to be more proactive in helping this child set reasonable goals and handle frustrations.

"It's wonderful when the teacher welcomes a parent's perspective," says one parent, Denise Brooks. "There were times in other years when I had things I wanted to tell my child's teacher, but I was afraid the teacher would think, 'Oh, here's a crazy mother coming in bothering me when it's such a busy time of year.'" When a teacher initiates these early meetings, parents feel that what they have to say is valued. "It's like the teacher's setting out the welcome mat," Denise says.

Taking the time to meet with parents at the beginning of the year smoothes the way for the rest of the year, says Susan. If the first conference is positive and filled with an atmosphere of mutual interest and respect, then if any problems come up later, parents and teachers will be more likely to work cooperatively to resolve them.

Here are some tips from Susan on holding beginning-of-the-year conferences:

Make it easy for families to come

In her invitation letter, Susan asks parents to choose a meeting day and to name a time before or after school that works for them. If they can't meet before or after school, Susan tries to find times during the school day. For example, parents sometimes come when the class is at a special, when Susan can meet with a parent without interruptions.

Spotlight:
The First
Parent
Conference

Make contact with every family

If a parent doesn't respond to the invitation, Susan sends a second note. If a parent sets up a time but doesn't show up, she sends a note suggesting another time. If that doesn't work, she makes a phone call and holds the hopes and dreams conference by phone. "I really try to make contact with every parent because I think it's just that important," she says.

Keep the meetings manageable for the teacher

By keeping the meetings short—they don't need to be long to be meaningful—Susan is able to have two or three per day without lengthening her day too much. Typically she has one meeting before school and one or two after school. With a class of about twenty-five children, she can talk to all parents in two weeks.

Show real interest in what parents have to say

Respectful, active listening is the most important way to show genuine interest. To further reassure parents that she's taking their goals seriously, Susan keeps every family's hopes and dreams sheet on file as documentation. She reassures parents that at the November conference, they'll talk about the child's progress toward the goals. At the November conference, she also invites parents to think about whether they would like to revise the goals based on the child's progress, the curriculum, or other factors.

Spotlight:

Healthy Homework

Third and Fourth Grades
Southern Aroostook Community School
Dyer Brook, Maine

Homework used to be an exasperation in April Bates's multi-age third-fourth grade class in Dyer Brook, Maine. Every day half a dozen students would show up at school without their homework. Another half a dozen would show up with it half done or barely started. April got after the noncompleters. She insisted, persisted, tried to hold every student to the same high standards. But nothing changed. Assignments remained undone. Children, parents, and teacher stayed frustrated. The sad state of homework continued—until April tried a new approach that put students' and their families' individual homework needs and tolerances squarely into the equation.

Chapter Two

"Homework has to be healthy for the whole family if it's to be successful," says April. Now, before assigning a single piece of homework, she engages students and all the parents in a discussion, asking about their past experiences with homework, explaining the purposes of homework, and helping parents know how best to help their children with assignments. Throughout the year, communication about homework continues, with adjustments made for individual children and families as needed.

Talking with children about homework

During the first six weeks of school, before any homework is assigned, April asks the children: "How many of you have had homework before?" "Why do you think teachers ask students to do homework?" "What has homework been like for you so far? Hard? Easy?" and "What do you like or not like about homework?"

She next talks with the children about what they need to have at home to do homework successfully, such as a designated place and time. She also goes over when to ask for help, whom to ask, and how to ask.

Then the class brainstorms possible problems that could get in the way of doing homework—everything from having after-school sports, to forgetting what the assignment was. For every possible problem, the children brainstorm possible solutions. If you have an after-school activity that conflicts with homework time, the solution might be to do the homework before or after. If you forget what the assignment was, maybe you can call up a "homework buddy" to ask. April writes all the possible problems and solutions on an easel chart for everyone to see. In a typical year the chart might look something like this:

Possible Homework Problems and Solutions to Try

**Spotlight:
Healthy
Homework**

What if you have homework and:	You could:
You don't know what the assignment is?	Call a homework buddy to ask.
You don't get it?	Try asking parents or siblings, or call a homework buddy.
The TV is on?	Ask to turn it off. Or ask for a quiet time and place.
It feels like work?	Just do it. Deal with it. It's your job.
The house is noisy?	Talk with your family about finding a quiet time and place.
You have company?	Schedule a homework time before or after. Or excuse yourself for awhile to do homework.
You have something fun to do?	Do your homework before or after the fun thing.
You don't have the materials you need?	Have a toolbox at home with pencil, paper, markers, crayons, etc. (Ms. Bates will help you put one together if you ask.)

Talking with parents about homework

Next it's time to talk with the parents. At the first parent conference of the year in early October, still before any homework is assigned, April asks parents about their children's history with homework. Some parents report all smooth sailing; others relate stories of having to remind their children five or six times to get to work, or of children breaking down in tears over homework. This is all important background for April.

After each meeting, she types up a page of notes, including the family's and child's strengths, constraints, and challenges that might affect homework success. This documentation, along with other information gathered as the year progresses, serves as her reference for individualizing homework assignments as needed.

Indeed, the idea that not all students have to do the same homework is an important one in April's homework philosophy. To her, the purpose of homework is for children to practice and build on what they learned at school and to develop the ability to work independently. But not all children are at the same place in their learning and their readiness for independent work. "I have four reading groups and two math groups in the class. If we accept that children's work at school should be individualized, and that homework should be an extension of schoolwork, then we need to individualize their homework, too," she says.

**Chapter
Two**

Clarifying parents' roles

At the October conference, April also reviews with parents the purpose of homework and offers some tips on helping a child with assignments. For example, she suggests that when a child needs help, parents offer just that—help—instead of doing the work for the child. "Parents could say something like, 'You try one question. Let me see what you're doing, and let's go from there.'"

Importantly, she asks parents to notice how long it takes their child to do the assignments. Third graders are to do no more than thirty minutes of homework a day; fourth graders no more than forty-five. "I ask parents to stop their child at thirty minutes or forty-five minutes depending on the grade, even if the child isn't finished," she says. To her way of thinking, children that age shouldn't be asked to do more, and if children can't finish in that amount of time even though they're working diligently, it's her job to try to understand why and then make the appropriate adjustments, not the children's job to work longer.

Parent Karen Rockwell likes that approach. Besides homework, there are chores, family time, and important downtime that compete for her son Eric's after-school hours. Keeping homework to forty-five minutes allows for all that to happen, she says.

At the first conference, parents are also shown the list of possible homework obstacles and possible solutions that the children brainstormed in class. "I liked seeing that list because it lets me know what they discussed," says Karen. She especially appreciated the way the solutions emphasized children trying to solve problems themselves—for example, by contacting their homework buddy to clarify what an assignment is—rather than immediately relying on their parents to fix things. "It makes them more independent, which is something I want for Eric," she says.

April also sends a letter to parents that gives some homework helping tips. A sample is shown on the facing page.

Spotlight: Healthy Homework

Homework slip

Only after building this foundation does April begin giving homework assignments. An important element then—one that encourages continuous school-home communication—is the daily homework slip. (See sample on page 57.) Children write their assignment for the evening on the sheet and take it home for their parents to sign. There's room on the sheet for a comment from parents, and many take advantage of it.

Sometimes the comments are a celebration: "Wow, he's getting it!" one parent wrote. Often they're informative: "He was really frustrated. He wanted to finish the assignment but couldn't. He needs more help with math word problems" or "We had a family emergency. She couldn't do her homework."

"These comments are really helpful to me," says April. "If the homework isn't done, I know why. If a child didn't understand something, it's helpful for me to know so we can revisit it in class. If a child couldn't finish the work in the allotted time, I know I gave too much."

Many families say the homework slips, by keeping them informed and in communication with the teacher, help them take an active role in their children's education. Melissa Porter, whose son Dylan was a third grader in April's class, says, "With the slips, I knew exactly what work he needed to do every day without having to ask him. I was on top of things, and he knew I was on top of things, and that was good for him. There was no way for him to slip through the cracks."

[Date]

Dear Parents,

We've been talking in class about homework, including why we have homework and what can help us do homework successfully. My goal is to keep homework purposeful and reasonable. I believe homework should never be a burden to the child or the family.

I have the following main purposes in assigning homework: to provide children with the opportunity to practice and improve their skills; and to teach children responsibility, self-discipline, independence, perseverance, and time management.

You can help your child be successful with homework by encouraging positive homework habits right from the start. Here are some suggestions:

- Set aside a specific time each day for homework. The sooner after school, the better.

- Designate a place for doing homework, a place that's quiet and has few distractions.

- Support your child in doing the work but don't do it for him/her. For example, you might remind your child where or how to find an answer, but try not to jump in to give the answer. (All homework will be on something we have already gone over in class.)

Please contact me if you have any questions or comments. I look forward to a year of successful homework!

Sincerely,

[Teacher's name]

Chapter Two

The second conference in December:
Check-in and problem solving

Homework is again a topic at the second conference in early December, when April talks with parents about whether the amount and type of homework needs adjusting. Parents also are given three choices at this time regarding the homework slips: to continue receiving and signing the slip, to continue receiving the slip but not have to sign it, or to stop receiving the slip altogether. Most parents choose to continue receiving the slip, though some opt for not having to sign it every day.

The December conference is also a time to address any homework problems that a child and family may be having. Perhaps the child missed homework on several occasions since October. Perhaps homework is being done sloppily. April is careful to use language that asks rather than commands in these conversations. "How do you think homework is going so far?" she might ask. Usually the parent's assessment is similar to April's. "Not that great," the parent might answer, then proceed to offer the cause of the problem from their perspective. "Is there something different that we can be doing?" April would ask.

"I find this kind of language much more effective than telling parents what to do," she explains. Most of the time, she says, parents have good insight into what's causing the problem and come up with good solutions to try.

In the small number of cases in which families feel that homework is going smoothly when April feels it isn't, she listens to their perspective, then shares hers. "Here's what I'm noticing about Chris's homework," she might say, then describe her observations objectively. Only when the parent and teacher have reached a common understanding of the problem do they go on to talk about possible solutions.

Not perfection, but a positive experience

The new homework approach hasn't erased all homework-related problems. Each year a handful of students still have trouble completing their homework consistently. But perfection isn't the goal. The goal is for homework to be a positive experience for all involved. "I feel better about homework because everyone's more comfortable—students, parents, and myself," April says.

Many families agree. "It's a much more proactive than reactive approach," says parent Karen Rockwell. "The children, the parents, the teacher all know there's going to be homework, and everyone's figuring out how to do it successfully. It feels like a group effort."

**Spotlight:
Healthy
Homework**

Sample Homework Slip

	Monday	Tuesday	Wednesday	Thursday
Name: _____ **Week of** _____				
Math				
Reading				
Writing				
Spelling				
Science				
Social studies				
Other				
Parent comment and signature				
Teacher comment				

Chapter Two

Chapter Three

M*y older son read at age five. My younger son is five and a half and is still not reading. What's wrong with him?*

Parent of a kindergartner

Last year her handwriting was easy to read. Now it's tiny and impossible to read. Why is her writing getting worse?

Parent of a second grader

I can't believe her behavior. She used to be so quiet and sweet. Now she's challenging everything, saying things aren't fair. What should we do?

Parent of a fourth grader

Children go through dramatic changes physically, cognitively, and socially as they grow. When adults understand these patterns of change, they can be much more effective in supporting children's learning. Longtime teacher and principal Chip Wood writes, "Children's developmental needs should be the foundation for every choice we make in our classrooms and schools." (Wood 1997, 1) A corollary to this statement is that children's developmental needs should be a foundation for how parents support their children's learning in school.

Many parents, however, have little knowledge of child development. They often don't know the cognitive, social, or language characteristics that children commonly have at different ages and how those characteristics affect their learning process. Worse, many parents feel a lot of anxiety about their child because normal stages in children's development look to them like problems, and normal differences in development among children look like deficiencies in the "slower" child.

Parents are left wondering: "Is my child normal?" "Should he be more advanced?" "Am I doing the right things as a parent?"

Teachers can help the situation by talking with parents about child development. When parents know what's normal for their child's age, they tend to worry less. When they have an idea of what their child will need in order to move to the next developmental stage, they're more likely to offer the appropriate supports, neither limiting the child's growth nor burdening the child with unrealistic expectations.

Key Ideas to Share with Parents

But isn't communicating about child development issues a huge task? It doesn't have to be. I've found that most parents don't want or need to know deep theory about child development or about what various researchers contributed to the field. They just need information in plain language about patterns in development that they might expect in their child, along with practical tips on how best to support their child at various stages of development. This chapter will offer some suggestions on communicating with parents about such topics.

Before going on, I want to note that in talking with parents about child development, my goal is not to change their parenting practices at home. My focus is on enabling parents to help their child with school. As a teacher, my expertise is in schooling, and my goal is to engage parents as partners in their child's school learning.

Key Ideas to Share with Parents

In talking with parents about child development, I've found it useful to share the following ideas:

- Typical developmental characteristics of children at their child's age

- How to respond to those characteristics

- The fact that all children develop at different rates

- The fact that children's development is uneven

I discuss each of these areas below. First, though, let me emphasize that the patterns of child development described in this chapter are broad generalizations, not rigid truths. Children's development and growth are influenced by factors such as their personality, health, and importantly, their culture and environment. What a child is capable of doing at each age, and what s/he is interested in or concerned about at each age, depend largely on what that child has been exposed to and is expected or encouraged to do. This means that children in different cultures and environments can develop in significantly different ways.

This is especially important to keep in mind as the U.S. school-age population becomes increasingly diverse in race, ethnicity, family structure, and other ways. The "typical" child development characteristics I mention in this chapter are derived from child development research done on predominantly White, European and U.S. middle-class children, combined with decades of observation of U.S. school children by practicing teachers. While the resulting information is valuable, it should not be presented to parents as truths that apply to all children. It's important that we acknowledge to parents that these broad generalizations of child development may not take into full account differences among racial and ethnic groups, or among families with dissimilar family structures or incomes. We can invite parents to apply their own insights about their family culture as they consider these broad generalizations. And as teachers, we would be wise to learn continuously from our students' parents, from our students themselves, and from resources available in the field about the development of children in various cultures and environments. (See the box below.)

Chapter Three

Culture and Child Development: Helpful Resources

Comer, James P., and Alvin F. Poussaint. 1992. *Raising Black Children.* New York: Plume Books.

Greenfield, Patricia M., and Rodney R. Cocking, eds. 1994. *Cross-Cultural Roots of Minority Child Development.* Hillsdale, NJ: Lawrence Erlbaum Associates.

Hale-Benson, Janice. 1986. *Black Children: Their Roots, Culture, and Learning Styles.* Baltimore: Johns Hopkins University Press.

Rogoff, Barbara. 2003. *The Cultural Nature of Human Development.* Reprint Edition. New York: Oxford University Press.

The typical developmental characteristics of the child's age

The first thing I communicate to parents is that at each age, children within a given culture tend to have common physical, cognitive, social, and language characteristics. To help parents understand the likely characteristics at their child's age, I give them handouts at back-to-school night. The handouts are based on information in the book *Yardsticks: Children in the Classroom Ages 4–14* by Chip Wood. They list the physical, social, language, and cognitive growth patterns that are most common among U.S. fourth graders, the grade that I teach. For example, language characteristics generally seen in nine-year-olds include "loves vocabulary and language play, baby-talk sometimes re-emerges, likes to use exaggeration." Likely cognitive characteristics of this age include "intellectually curious, able to think about the 'bigger world,' trouble grasping abstractions such as large numbers, long periods of time, and great expanses of space."

Key Ideas to Share with Parents

But I don't give parents just one handout. I give them *four*—one for eight-year-olds, one for nine-year-olds, one for ten-year-olds, and one for eleven-year-olds—even though the majority of fourth graders are nine or ten. I do this because child developmental patterns can vary given the diversity of the U.S. school-age population and to make the crucial point that children's *developmental* age may not match their *chronological* age. For example, a child who is chronologically ten may exhibit behaviors more commonly seen in eleven-year-olds and vice versa. Also, children's behaviors and needs do not suddenly change on their birthdays. When a child moves into a new age, it usually takes the child several months to consistently exhibit the behaviors of the new age. For example, a child who turns nine in September may continue to show typical eight-year-old behaviors into December. Similarly, a child who is a few months away from turning eleven may already be showing a few common eleven-year-old characteristics. When it comes to learning, I tell parents, it's the child's *developmental* age that matters most.

With the handouts distributed, I briefly highlight a few of the developmental characteristics of each of the four ages, reminding parents that these are broad generalizations that may not apply exactly to every child. In choosing which characteristics to highlight, I focus on a few that I have observed in the children in this class and that many parents therefore are probably noticing, too. For example, I often speak about how it's common for nine-year-olds to be critical, worried, full of complaints. As we talk, there are chuckles and affirmations of "Oh yeah!" around the circle. As the discussion continues and parents realize that they and their child are not the only ones going through this phase, I see their demeanors change. Many breathe a sigh of relief as they come to understand that their nine-year-old is perfectly normal, and that they are not bad parents.

How to respond to children's developmental characteristics

Next I talk about how children's developmental characteristics affect what we do in the classroom, which can give parents ideas for similar things to try at home. For example, continuing with the "worried and full of complaints" characteristics, I tell parents that I try to respond with empathy. It's tempting to try to help a child feel better by diminishing the problem. "It's really not such a big deal" or "Oh, you don't really feel that way," adults often tell a child. I explain that often what children really want, however, is for adults to listen and understand how they're feeling. So I often respond to a child's complaints by saying, "It sounds like you're really worried about your math test" or "You sound worried that you won't have anyone to play with at recess and you'll be all alone." I tell parents that sometimes humor, fantasy, or lightheartedness can be helpful in defusing some of that seriousness. For example, adults could say, "I wish I could wave a magic wand and make all of your homework disappear!"

At the same time that I suggest some ways to be supportive, I also make the point that "development is not an excuse." For example, I let parents know that just because it's common for many nine-year-olds to be critical, that doesn't mean teachers allow these children to go around criticizing everyone and everything. It does mean we acknowledge that tendency in children this age and work with them to find the good in things. And we teach them to express their views in less critical ways. Again, hearing this seems to help parents get some ideas to try at home.

In talking with parents about child development, I'm careful not to dwell only on the challenging traits that children tend to display at certain ages. It's also important that parents appreciate the strengths that come with their child's stage of development. I often tell parents, for example, that because children around the age of nine look hard for explanations of facts—how things work and why things happen as they do—this is a great age for scientific exploration. It's also an age when children take pride in finished work, so they can be expected to work hard on a report, a project, or a model. I encourage parents to support such endeavors in their children.

Throughout the rest of the year, I continue to find opportunities to share developmental information with parents. Here are some opportunities for such sharing:

Classroom newsletter

About once a month, I include in my classroom newsletter a small blurb about a developmental issue that I'm seeing in students or a reminder of some of the growth patterns we talked about at back-to-school night. It may be a paragraph or two from a magazine or newspaper, or something I wrote myself. Regardless, I always make sure the language is easy for busy parents to read and absorb quickly, and I give an idea or two that parents can consider for supporting their children.

Here are samples about two different ages:

About seven-year-olds

Key Ideas to Share with Parents

Seven-year-olds can be extremely sensitive and moody. They may sulk a lot and often get depressed. They often like to spend long periods alone, reading, listening to music, or playing with a toy. When playing with a group, they're likely to suddenly say, "I quit!" and stomp off, but it's often not because they didn't get their way. More likely it's because they feel they're not as good at the game or project as others. If you're seeing these tendencies in your child, you can help by protecting his/her feelings. Avoid teasing, joking, or laughing at your child for a wrong answer or silly idea. Never use sarcasm, which can be harmful to children of any age and especially painful to seven-year-olds.

About eleven-year-olds

Eleven tends to be an age of big changes. Many children this age seem to be challenging everything they assumed about the world up to now, including adult rules and boundaries that they used to accept without question. They can come across as quite rude when they're challenging everything like this. Yet they're often genuinely surprised when adults take offense and are easily embarrassed when adults correct or reprimand them.

Remember, the fact that this is typical behavior doesn't give your child license to be rude to you or anyone else. So if your child makes a rude comment, let her/him know that this is unacceptable behavior, but try to do it in a way that lets your child "save face," even in seemingly innocuous situations. For example, avoid correcting your child in front of her/his peers. Find another time or place to talk about the incident.

Conferences

Conferences are another opportunity to communicate about child development. These one-on-one times allow parents to raise questions unique to their child or to share perspectives about child development and child raising in their culture or their family's specific circumstances. To invite these conversations, I sometimes take out the child development handouts I showed at back-to-school night. I give parents a few minutes to look through the handouts and see if there are any developmental characteristics that they want to talk about. I listen carefully, for these are precious opportunities to gain insights about the family, insights that will help me teach the child more effectively.

Often parents raise concerns about some behavior they're seeing in their child. When this happens, it's crucial to respond with empathy, even if we feel that the behavior is developmentally normal. Amy Wade, a school counselor at Canandaigua Primary School in Rochester, New York, says it helps to begin by validating the parent's concern before offering further comments or suggestions. She tells of the parents who complained about their young six-year-old being oppositional. "Even when we tell her many times not to do something, she continues to do it," the parents said. After listening a while, Amy realized that the child's behavior was a classic example of the opposition and impulsiveness that teachers see in so many young six-year-olds. But rather than saying so right away, she began with, "That kind of behavior can be hard to live with." Only after offering this validation of the parents' feelings did she explain that the child's behaviors are considered quite normal, and only then did she suggest some ways the parents could work with the child.

Conferences are also a time for me to raise any developmental issue that I may want to discuss with the parents. For example, I may talk about how eight-year-old Cate often turns in work that she has not proofread or taken the time to do carefully. Turning to the handout on eight-year-olds, I point to "Speedy, works in a hurry." I remind the parents that this is something that teachers commonly see in children this age. However, reinforcing the idea that development is not an excuse, I suggest that at school and home we can help Cate work on slowing down and proofreading her work by giving her brief, matter-of-fact, and encouraging reminders. I offer parents some examples, such as "Interesting story you've got here. Remember to proofread it before handing it in" or "Finished? You have five more minutes. You can go back and check those computations carefully."

Dropoffs, pickups, and other brief encounters

In the course of the year, we usually have various opportunities to talk informally with parents about child development. Often the best times are dropoffs and pickups and times when we make positive news phone calls or send periodic postcards. (See Chapter 4.)

My daughter's day care teacher was a master at this kind of informal communication:

> "Riley likes her routine," she commented with a smile one afternoon when I came to pick up my daughter.
>
> "Oh, I know. She certainly makes that clear to me when I try to change it in any way," I replied.
>
> "Developmentally, that's very typical of the two-year-olds I see. They like predictability and routine. They like to know what's coming before it comes," the teacher said in a friendly voice.
>
> She went on, "We make sure we give the children plenty of warning before we change their routine at school. Once they know a change is coming, they can begin to make the shift in their brains and make the transition more smoothly."

Key Ideas to Share with Parents

In less than a minute, the teacher did three powerful things: First, she communicated a piece of relevant developmental information about my daughter. Second, she let me know that this characteristic is normal for my daughter's age, relieving my anxiety about it. Third, she gave me a practical, easy strategy that I could use at home to handle this characteristic.

If I'd had a concern or a different take on my daughter's behavior, the fact that the teacher made a comment about behavior would have given me an opportunity to speak up. Her smile, friendly voice, and easygoing manner would have made me feel safe to say what was on my mind.

Elementary school teachers can do the same with the parents of their students. To the parent of a five-year-old going on six, we might say, "Mia's getting a little older and braver about experimenting. A lot of children this age are testing limits more." Perhaps the parent will say, "Tell me about it. She's getting so willful," or something similar. We can respond with something like, "At school we find that clear rules and consistent discipline can really help, though we don't use harsh discipline because we know the children are just trying to understand the limits." To the parent of a ten-year-old, we might say, "Kevin just beams when I comment on something helpful he did. We see this over and over in ten-year-olds: they love to be noticed and recognized for their efforts. Saying things like 'I see that you've...' or 'I notice you're...' can go a long way." (For more examples, see "Sample Language for Talking with Parents about Child Development" on page 70.)

Children develop at different rates

An important point to help families understand is that children don't all go through developmental stages at the same time or at the same rate. As obvious as it sounds, it's important to remind parents frequently that no two children are the same.

Maybe it's part of human nature to compare one's child to others. "Why isn't my child reading chapter books yet? So many of her friends are." "My child can do double digit division. Can yours?" "My friend's child could sit still for long periods of time by now. My child still can't. Is there something wrong with him?" Although the comparing comes from parents wanting to make sure their children are developing appropriately, it often brings forth a great deal of unnecessary anxiety. Often parents' biggest concerns are "Is my child normal?" and "Am I a bad parent?"

In almost all cases, the answers are "yes" and "no" respectively. It helps when teachers reassure parents of this over and over. It helps to remind parents that truly supporting their children includes appreciating the fact that different children develop at different rates. "Every child is unique," I tell parents. "Not all children potty train at two and a half, not all children learn to read at age six, not all children master multiplication tables by age ten, and that's okay."

Parents may appreciate hearing that the range of what's considered normal development can be wide. One ten-year-old might have some behaviors that are typical of most of her nine-year-old peers. Another might behave more like the eleven-year-olds. Both children are normal, yet their developmental ages span two years.

Children's growth is uneven

The final concept that's important for parents to understand is that children's growth is uneven. It's uneven in two ways. First, children may mature quickly in one area, such as cognitive ability, but more slowly in another, such as social competence or physical ability.

Second, children tend to have active periods in their development followed by quiet periods; and calm, compliant periods followed by fretful, moody periods. Sometimes development even seems to move backwards. There's a passage from Chip Wood's book *Yardsticks* which describes this phenomenon. I like to share it with parents:

> Growth is uneven. Like the seasons, the tides, the turning of the earth on itself and around the sun, the birth and death of stars, the music of the universe—there is an ebb and flow to life that is mystical and spiritual. Babies are calm at one time of day, fretful at another. Children are more compliant and obedient at one age, more resistant and difficult at others. Learning seems to come in spurts and be followed by periods of consolidation. Sudden spurts of physical growth are obvious, and are followed by periods of little physical change. This shifting back and forth is a normal part of the life cycle and appears to continue into adulthood. (Wood 1997, 27)

Parents seem to find comfort in this passage. It's a concept that many parents know when their children are young but forget when the children reach school age. One parent said, "I thought that once my child got out of the 'terrible twos' it would be smooth sailing from there on out, at least until she became a teenager." Parents often forget that their children are still going through enormous growth and development in the years between toddlerhood and adolescence. I find that parents appreciate being reminded of this fact.

Heads-Up: Preparing Parents for the Next Developmental Stage

As children grow and change throughout the year, it's helpful to give parents a heads-up on what developmental issues might be coming up for their child. One manageable way to do this is to send a letter home at the point in the year when most of the class seems to be moving into a new developmental stage.

To do this, teachers need to be attuned to where most children in the class are in their development. Although any given class will have a wide range of chronological and developmental ages, there usually is a span in which most of the children cluster. For example, in one fourth grade class most of the children might be young nines at the beginning of the year. Most likely, these children will still be more like eight- than nine-year-olds developmentally. In another fourth grade classroom most of the children might have been nine for quite a few months and be showing solid nine-year-old developmental characteristics.

By tuning in to what this dominant developmental age is in their classrooms, teachers can know when they might want to send a heads-up note to parents.

Preparing Parents for the Next Developmental Stage

If the majority of my class is developmentally eight at the beginning of the year, I know that as the second half of the year approaches, I'll want to prepare parents for the fact that their child will soon be developmentally nine. When that time comes, I send home another copy of the child development handout on nine-year-olds along with a brief note. The note explains that over the next few months, most children in the class will begin to exhibit many of the characteristics listed on the handout. I also remind parents that this is an age of great growth and, with it, some "growing pains." I reassure them that this does not mean there's something wrong with their child or with their approach to child raising.

Parents tend to like having this heads-up. They seem more able to support their children through the challenging issues attending certain ages when they know about them ahead of time.

An understanding of child development enriches all that we do with and for children. The more that we adults—teachers and parents—know about how children change and grow, the more effectively we can work together to support the children's learning.

Chapter Three

Spotlight:

Sample Language for
Talking with Parents about Child Development

When talking with parents about child development, you don't have to say a lot to convey a lot. Here's a three-step process for helping parents understand common developmental characteristics that they're noticing in their child:

1. Name and briefly define the characteristic. Be clear that the characteristic is common in children at this age.

2. Share one way in which you might adjust classroom practices when you see this characteristic. This helps parents understand your classroom practices and can give them ideas for similar things to do at home.

**Spotlight:
Language
for Talking
about Child
Development**

3. Keep in mind—and remind parents if necessary—that a child's developmental age may not always match her/his chronological age. A child who just turned ten, for example, might be developmentally like most nine-year-old peers for a few more months. During that time, it would be appropriate to interact with the child as if s/he were nine.

The chart on the next pages gives examples from Amy Wade, a counselor at Canandaigua Primary School in Canandaigua, New York.

(Note: The characteristics listed for each age are broad generalizations based on European and U.S. child development studies and observations of children in U.S. schools. Child developmental patterns may differ significantly in different cultures and environments.)

Age	A common developmental characteristic	Sample language
4	Can't sit still or pay attention very long	"Four-year-olds often need a lot of physical activity and can only sit still for short periods. I mix physical activity with sitting and listening. Several short sitting times work better than one long one."
5	Acts on one thing at a time	"It's common for five-year-olds to be very literal. What they see and hear is what they know. So they can only act on one thing at a time. Teachers therefore also focus on one thing at a time by keeping expectations clear and simple."
6	Highly competitive	"Six-year-olds often love to be first. To temper that, we try to have cooperative rather than competitive activities in the classroom. If we do have a competitive activity, we talk beforehand about what good sportsmanship looks and sounds like."
7	Sensitive and moody	"*Nobody likes me.* A lot of seven-year-olds think that. I try to be extra supportive and reassuring for this age. It helps to validate their feelings first, then make suggestions. *Sounds like you're feeling like no one likes you. Who would you like to sit with at lunch today? I'll help you ask that friend to join you.*"
8	Complains of being bored	"At school we see a lot of eight-year-olds with big ideas but not the organization to carry them out, and that can make them feel incapable. *I'm bored* can often really mean *things are too hard.* If this is the case, I help them get organized and break their work into manageable chunks."

Chapter Three

Spotlight: Language for Talking about Child Development

Age	A common developmental characteristic	Sample language
9	Serious and worries a lot	"Children this age often worry about lots of things: world events, family, friends. They constantly say things aren't fair. They take any criticism to heart. I try to offset some of this seriousness with a combination of humor, light-heartedness, and encouraging language."
10	Enjoys being noticed	"Most ten-year-olds like to be noticed. So I let them know that I noticed their positive behaviors: *I see you've worked diligently on this journal entry* or *You're working well together as a group today.*"
11	Easily embarrassed	"Many children this age are easily embarrassed or demoralized by even the most benign comment, so teachers try not to correct them in front of their peers. It's better to find a private time to talk."
12	Can't be bothered with small, everyday tasks	"Twelve-year-olds can be very responsible with important projects like raising money for a good cause. But often everyday things like doing their homework or straightening their lockers just aren't a priority. In class, we often discuss consequences for not meeting expectations on these small everyday tasks. Giving children this age a say in what the consequences should be can help them be more responsible."

Chapter Four

U*sually when your child
isn't having problems, you don't hear from the teacher. But my
daughter's teacher will call just to check in and tell about some little
thing he noticed my child doing. It makes me feel like he knows my child.*

Parent of a third grader

It means a lot to parents when teachers make contact just to check in and offer some small positive comment about their children. "Caitlyn said the most interesting thing in a book discussion this week, and she's remembering to raise her hand before talking," we might say, or "Temi wrote an exciting story. He's working hard on proofreading, too. I'm noticing capital letters and correct punctuation." Such a simple act, yet it makes a world of difference. When parents trust that the teacher knows and appreciates their child, they're much more likely to work collaboratively to support the child's education.

This positive approach is different from the traditional model of teacher-family relations, in which, other than the two required conferences of the year, teachers contact parents only when children are having difficulties. The problem with that model is that parents begin to equate any contact from the teacher with trouble. Any time there's a phone message from the teacher or a note sent home, parents immediately assume it's bad news. This form of communication does little to create a collaborative school-home relationship. In fact, it does just the opposite. Parents often get defensive and feel resentful that this is the only time they hear from their child's teacher.

As teachers, we don't intend for parents to feel this way. It's just that in our very hectic days, we're lucky to have time to sit down for a few minutes to eat lunch. Finding the time to reach out to families consistently can seem next to impossible. So we put off the phone calls and the notes until a problem comes up.

Yet it's enormously important to maintain regular positive communication with parents throughout the year. Over the years I've learned that contacting parents when nothing's wrong—contacting them just to share what's going on in our classroom and what their child is doing well—is not a frill, but the core of effective communication with families.

Reasons for Staying in Touch

Here are just some of the reasons it's so important to maintain regular, positive communication with parents:

Reasons for
Staying in
Touch

Methods of
Keeping in
Touch

It gives parents a window into their child's daily school life

Parents need to know what their child is studying and what else is going on in the classroom to be able to offer constructive help.

It sets a positive tone for school–home communication

If our communication with parents is rather sporadic, mostly centered on negative issues, and somewhat accusatory in tone, they'll likely respond the same way. But if we're supportive and encouraging, parents are more apt to be supportive and encouraging of us as well.

It builds a trusting relationship with parents

Frequent positive communication lays the groundwork for a productive, trusting school–home relationship. Once that trust is in place, it's possible for the teacher and parent to work collaboratively on difficult issues that might come up during the year.

Methods of Keeping in Touch

But how do we keep up positive communication without feeling overwhelmed? I used to think it couldn't be done. I have since learned, however, that staying in touch doesn't necessarily take a lot of time. Here are just a few ideas that are manageable for teachers while giving parents the information they need to be connected to their child's school life.

In deciding which methods to use, consider what you will realistically sustain and what will be comfortable for your particular group of parents.

Positive news phone calls

Keeping in touch could begin with something as simple as picking up the phone when you notice something positive in a child. The child doesn't have to have accomplished some big feat. Winchester, New Hampshire music teacher Atsuko Imanishi often calls parents simply to say, "I noticed your child kept the beat for a long time today" or "Your child has really enjoyed singing lately."

Sharing successes with parents is easier if teachers develop a habit of recording their observations of students. You might write down your observations of just one or two children a day, covering the whole class in a few weeks, and pulling from these notes in communicating with parents.

Many teachers set up a system to ensure that all families get called. One possibility is to call everyone once a grading period, so that each family gets three or four calls a year. When a child does something interesting or helpful, worked hard on something, or made progress on a skill or project, call to let the parent know. Then, check off the child's name in your grade book so you know you've made at least one call to that family that grading period.

Jeremy Nellis, a K–1 teacher in Minneapolis, sets up phone calls at specific, scheduled times. At the beginning of the year he asks parents to name a day of the week that's convenient for them to take an early morning or evening call from him. He then calls them every other week on their chosen day. He reports something positive about the child, updates them on the class's thematic units and upcoming events, and invites questions. "It's created a very open form of communication with families," he says.

Whether a teacher calls parents every few months or every few weeks, spontaneously or according to a schedule, it's the positive nature of the contact that matters. "I've only had two phone calls this year," says one parent in early spring. "That feels enough. Those two calls stay with me."

Some teachers worry that by regularly telling parents positive things about their child, they might be giving a skewed picture of how the child is really doing in school, particularly if the child is having difficulties. Remember that this is not the only time teachers talk with parents. As teachers, we certainly want to use the full range of communication channels available to give parents a complete picture of their child's progress.

I want to acknowledge that it is easier to find complimentary things to say about some children than others. In all of our classrooms, there are children who perform a hundred acts of kindness, do lots of beautiful work, and stay organized, all of which we would readily comment on. There are also children who struggle and resist, who do sloppy work or don't do work at all, who test our patience and push our buttons, leaving us searching for anything positive to say about them. The children in the latter group, however, are the ones whose parents need to hear positive comments the most. These parents, and the children themselves, probably benefit from positive feedback more than anyone because they're so used to hearing all the negative things. I have found that the more I focus on the positive with these children, the more open they and their parents are to working on difficult issues.

Methods of Keeping in Touch

The child doesn't have to be perfect in something before we report it to the family. "Robbie is continuing to work on using friendly words to say he disagrees," we might say, or "Takako is showing progress in doing independent research." No matter what difficulties a child has, I believe there is always something good, something positive, we can find in every child. We just have to take the time to look.

Periodic postcards

Postcards can work much the same way as phone calls. At the beginning of the year, buy or make enough postcards for the year, depending on how often you plan to send them out. You can have students write their addresses on the cards. Then, when you have something positive to share with a family, jot it down on a postcard and drop it in the mail. Parents have told me how much they enjoy the surprise of getting these postcards at unexpected times. Often the postcards go onto the refrigerator and are savored for months.

On the facing page is a sample postcard, front and back.

Regular emails

If parents have easy access to computers, another way to keep in touch is through email. One advantage of email is that the same message can be sent to separated parents, to a parent and a specialist working with the child, or any group of people involved in the child's school learning. Another convenience of email is that they're easy to reply to, which can encourage parents to write back with questions and comments.

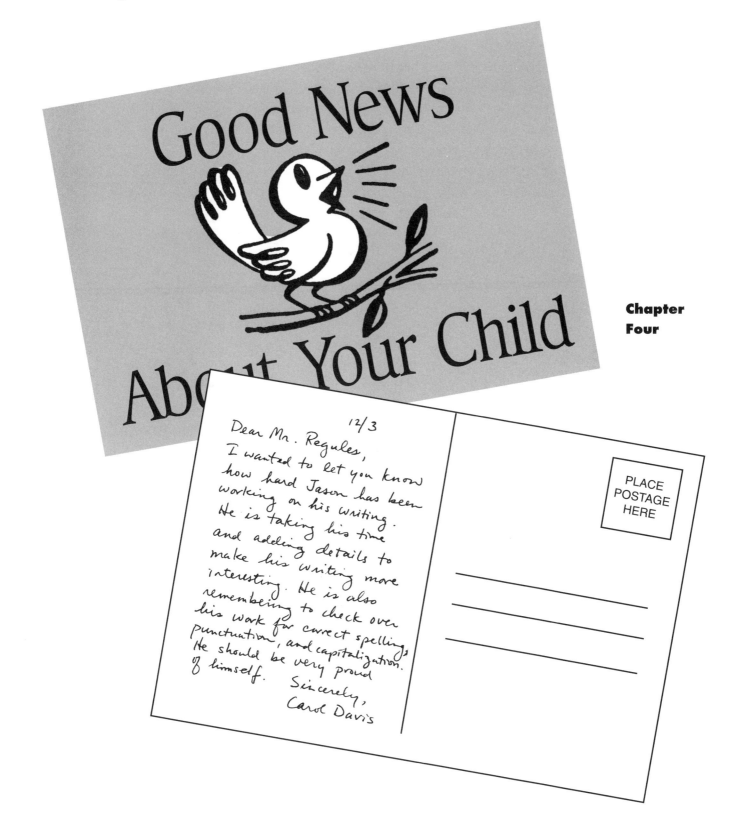

Chapter Four

12/3

Dear Mr. Regules,
I wanted to let you know how hard Jason has been working on his writing. He is taking his time and adding details to make his writing more interesting. He is also remembering to check over his work for correct spelling, punctuation, and capitalization. He should be very proud of himself.
Sincerely,
Carol Davis

PLACE POSTAGE HERE

Some teachers use email to send their classroom newsletter as a group message to all parents. Fifth grade teacher Ken Kowalski in South Brunswick, New Jersey, who uses email extensively to communicate with parents, finds that because it's so easy for readers to "reply to all," these group emails sometimes have the welcome effect of encouraging parents to talk with each other and strengthen a sense of community among themselves.

Methods of Keeping in Touch

Email Newsletter to Families

Here's a sample email newsletter from fifth grade teacher Ken Kowalski of Brunswick Acres School, South Brunswick, New Jersey:

Dear Parents,

Everyone came in ready this morning and we started Morning Meeting right away. We did a skip greeting. I started by greeting the second person on my right, skipping one person. Immediately everyone saw the pattern. Tomorrow we will greet the third person on our right, skipping two people. Everyone really watches to see how the pattern moves around the circle. The Sharing during Morning Meeting this month is very interesting. Students are sharing something that they did to make you, their parents, proud.

Reading groups continue to go very well. Thanks to help from several of you, our SRA is really moving along. We have also continued our new research project and our vocabulary work during reading time in the morning. Reading group discussions continue to reveal new strategies as students talk about what they do when they read. The discussions also reveal new aspects of their creativity. This morning, students were using unusual ways to share their understanding of the chapters. You might want to ask your child about this.

We are finishing up the chapter on division in math. We did the chapter review yesterday and started the chapter test today. We will continue exploring division and multiplication in a variety of ways.

Yesterday the students went to the library to find books for independent reading, and today they completed a funny and colorful project in art.

Have an enjoyable weekend.
Ken Kowalski

Weekly or biweekly newsletters

Traditional paper newsletters about classroom happenings remain an effective way to keep in positive touch with families. "That newsletter is important to me," says Annette Tirado, mother of a fourth grader. Even though her full-time job keeps her from attending many school meetings and events, she feels informed of her child's school life largely because of the newsletters, she says.

Yet teachers as a whole have mixed feelings about classroom newsletters. While many enjoy writing them, others groan at the thought. Some teachers report that parents read newsletters eagerly; others say parents leave them ignored for days on the kitchen table. I myself used to put hours into writing newsletters, only to find out later that most parents didn't read them.

I've since realized that part of my problem was that I was putting too much information into my newsletters. They were overwhelming for me to write and overwhelming for parents to read after a long, busy day.

Newsletters took on a whole different feel, however, when I began sending simple "Ask me about…" newsletters, an idea that I got from a group of teachers at a workshop: As part of closing circle at the end of each school day, the students gather for a few minutes to share aloud what they learned that day, whether in the academic or social realm. I record their reflections. Once a week, I choose the most interesting of these named learnings and type them up in the form of questions for parents to ask their children. At the bottom of the page I jot down any brief notes and reminders that I want to give to parents. On the following page is an example from one week.

Parents like the "Ask me about…" format because it not only gives them a picture of what their children are doing in school, but it also gives them specific language for engaging their children in conversation. As a teacher, I like it because I can get parents' help in reinforcing children's learning while keeping the newsletter work manageable for myself.

Chapter Four

Methods of Keeping in Touch

Ask me about...

- How a lever works

- The process we learned for solving conflicts

- The story I'm publishing in writers' workshop

- How the pioneers built their homes

- What a quadrilateral is and what examples of quadrilaterals we have in our home

- Ideas we learned for what to do when someone is bothering us

- The new greeting we learned in Morning Meeting this week

- One of the new reading strategies we worked on this week (ask me to read a page in my book to show how to use this strategy)

Dear Parents:

If you have not yet returned a permission slip for your child to take part in next week's field trip, please do so by this Thursday. Thank you!

Carol Davis

Daily or weekly "exit pass"

Like an "Ask me about..." newsletter, an "exit pass" is something that can help parents stay informed about classroom life while having a productive conversation with their children. Sometime each day or week, every student receives an exit pass that s/he fills out before leaving for the day. The pass, perhaps a brightly colored half sheet of paper, has a series of conversation prompts on it. The child chooses one prompt to complete and takes the sheet home to share with his/her parents. If the teacher wants to communicate something else to the parents, s/he could attach a note. Here's an example of an exit pass:

Exit Pass

My favorite part of today was _____

One thing I learned today was _____

One thing I liked today was _____

Today I was proud that I _____

A way I solved a problem today was _____

A way I helped someone today was _____

Your own idea: _____

Weekly work folders

Another way of maintaining communication with parents is to regularly send children's work home along with a quick note. I use a system called "Thursday Papers." Students keep a folder of schoolwork from the week, which they take home every Thursday to show their parents. Inside the folder is also a bright gold slip of paper with a space for me to write a comment and a space for the parents to write a comment.

In my comment, I always find something positive to say about the child: "Hayden has been using friendly words when asking to borrow something from a classmate" or "Cristal worked hard on her chapter book this week." Whenever possible, I try to connect my comment to the goal or hope that the parents named for their child at our hopes and dreams conference at the beginning of the year. If there's anything else I need parents to know that does not require a more in-depth note or phone call, I also write that on the slip.

After the child goes over the papers with the parents, the parents write a comment on the slip if they wish, then sign the slip. "I can see that John is really taking his time to write neatly on all of this work," one parent wrote. Often parents respond with a question, such as "Can you suggest some fun ways to practice multiplication with Tina at home?"

The child brings the folder back to school on Friday, when I read the parents' comments. I then keep the slips of paper as part of the documentation of the child's progress throughout the year.

Here's a sample Thursday Papers slip:

Methods of Keeping in Touch

Thursday Papers

Child's name: *Gail Goldberg*

Teacher's comment:
Gail has remembered to turn her homework in every day this week!

Parent's comment:
WE HAVE WORKED HARD TO SET UP A REGULAR HOMEWORK TIME. GAIL HAS BEEN TAKING THE RESPONSIBILITY TO GET STARTED ON HER HOMEWORK BY HERSELF. THANKS FOR YOUR HELP WITH THIS.

Parent's signature: *Helen Goldberg*   Date: *11/26*

Parents seem to like this form of communication. They appreciate seeing their children's work consistently and they enjoy hearing positive things about their child.

If writing a comment about each child every week feels overwhelming, the answer is to start small. When I started using Thursday Papers, the communication form had only a place for parents to write comments; I didn't write any comments myself. A while later, I started commenting on six or seven students each week, knowing that as the weeks went by, every student will have gotten comments. Soon, observing and picking one positive thing to share about each child became an easier habit, so I expanded to writing comments about five or six students each day. By Thursday, I had a comment for every child in the class.

A variation on Thursday Papers is to include with each child's folder a "Pluses and Wish" form, an idea I got from teacher Sally Kitts. On the form, the child offers a quick reflection of the week's work by writing two "pluses" (things s/he did well) and one "wish" (an area to improve on). The teacher also writes two pluses and one wish about the child's work. After the parents look through the folder with the child, they add their two pluses and one wish. When the folder comes back to school, the teacher reads the parents' pluses and wish and keeps the slips of paper as documentation of the child's progress.

(For more about sharing students' work with parents, see Chapter 7.)

Videos

For teachers who have access to a video camera and can set one up easily in the classroom, making short videotapes for parents might be an effective way of keeping in touch, particularly with parents who don't read English well or simply prefer watching a video over reading.

Videos can be used to provide a short introduction of yourself as a teacher, to update parents on what's happening in the classroom, and to share the successes of individual children with their parents. If it's a video meant for all parents, make a few copies and have the children take turns taking them home. If it's a video meant for an individual parent, simply have that child take it home.

(For more about videos, see Chapter 5.)

Develop an Approach That Works for You

There are many other ways to communicate with parents. You can develop an approach that works for you and your particular group of families. Start small, experiment, and keep the goals in mind: to let parents know what their child is learning in school, to set a positive tone for school-home communication, and to build a trusting relationship with parents.

Spotlight:

Weekend Family Message Journals

First and Second Grade
Penn Valley Elementary School
Levittown, Pennsylvania

Spotlight:
Weekend
Family
Message
Journals

"Whenever I ask my son what he did at school, he just says 'Nothing,'" one parent laments. "I ask him how was recess, he says 'Okay.' I ask what he liked about school today, he says 'I don't know.'"

It's a familiar complaint among parents. They want to talk with their children about school, but their attempts to start conversations go nowhere.

First and second grade teacher Sue DeMeglio of Penn Valley Elementary School in Levittown, Pennsylvania, wanted to help families break through this "Nothing/Okay/I don't know" barrier. At the same time, she wanted to understand her students' families better. And, she was looking for ways to help her students improve their language arts skills. She found the answer to all three in weekend family message journals, an adaptation of an idea from ReadWriteThink, a website sponsored by the International Reading Association, the National Council of Teachers of English, and the MarcoPolo Education Foundation. (www.readwritethink.org)

Every week the students wrote a short letter to their parents about something they did in school that week: "I played with Kelly at recess" or "We played soccer and I scored a goal" or "We are learning to make graphs." Drawings often accompanied the words. All letters were written in sturdy notebooks meant to last the whole year.

Each Friday, the children took the journals home. Over the weekend, their parents wrote a short letter back in the same notebook. The students brought their notebooks back to school on Mondays and could take turns sharing their parents' letters with the class during the week if they wanted to.

The idea, which Sue believes can be adapted for older elementary grades as well, proved popular with parents. "I always looked forward to getting the letters," says parent Nancy Poploskie, "and my son couldn't wait to read what I wrote."

Not only did the children's letters help launch fruitful conversations about specific happenings at school, but they helped parents reinforce or expand on classroom lessons at home. One week Nancy's son William wrote, "We mixed solids and liquids," which led the parent and child to continue the experiment at home, mixing sugar and water, spices and water, baking soda and vinegar, to see what would happen.

The journaling also stimulated conversations between Nancy and the teacher that helped Nancy better understand the curriculum and classroom practices. When William wrote one week, "I liked studying geometry," Nancy thought, "Geometry? Isn't that something you do in tenth grade?" She asked Sue about it and learned that the first and second graders were exploring shapes, lines, and symmetry that would pave the way for more advanced, formal geometry later.

For teachers, this kind of journaling can provide a valuable glimpse into families' priorities and interests. Sue recalls one mother, in writing back to her child, saying how helpful the child had been with the family's new baby. "I had kind of forgotten about the baby," says Sue. "Her letter helped me remember." It reminded her that the family's routine had no doubt changed as a result of the new baby and to keep that in mind when working with them.

For the children, the journaling provided obvious academic and social benefits. It was a chance not only to practice writing, but to write for an immediate, real-life purpose. Reading their parents' responses and then reading them aloud to the class provided further literacy practice. Additionally, by sharing the journals, classmates could let each other know about their families, an important way for the children to feel more understood.

As the year progressed, the letters became a tangible documentation of the children's growth. Letters that consisted of one or two sentences early in the year often grew into full-pagers containing detail and elaboration. Spelling improved. Correct punctuation appeared. William began asking questions in his letters. "Dear Mom, Mrs. DeMeglio is reading *The Dragons are Singing Tonight*. We wrote about being in a castle. Do you like working in a library?" The change, from a young child who can only think about himself to a more mature child who can consider other people and their feelings, was moving for Nancy. She might not have had such a clear documentation of that growth had it not been for the student-parent letter writing, she says.

On the following pages are several letters between William and his mom.

**Chapter
Four**

**Spotlight:
Weekend
Family
Message
Journals**

2-20-03

Dear Mom,

We are learning about graphs. On 100th day we wrote a paper about going 100 miles. The big mas had to do two tests.

Your son

William

2-23-03

Dear William,

What kind of things are you graphing? If you went 100 miles from home where do you think you would be? I can't wait until you write me again.

Love,

Mom

**Spotlight:
Weekend
Family
Message
Journals**

3-6-03

Dear mom,

Our animal reports

are coming along

good. I am on my good

copy. On thursday we

leaned adout frickshin.

3-8-03

Dear William,

What animal are you doing your report on? My guess would be a giraffe.

I think the way Mrs. DeMeglio taught you about friction was neat. I wouldn't have thought of it.
Love,
Mom

For teachers who want to try weekend family message journals, here are some tips:

Introduce the activity carefully to children

Sue began by reading with the class the book *The Jolly Postman* by Janet and Allan Ahlberg. That became a springboard for talking about what a letter is and why people write letters.

She then told the children they would be writing letters to their parents to tell about things they did at school. Together, the class brainstormed possible topics if they were writing to their parents that week. Their ideas included everything from what happened at recess to what the guest artist did with them. The list was posted on a wall in case children needed some ideas later for their letters.

Model letter writing for the children

On an easel chart, Sue modeled by writing a letter to her daughter, carefully using the conventional letter-writing format and asking the children to notice it. She also thought aloud for the children to hear: "Hmm, what could I tell my daughter about school this week? Let me look at the list of topics we brainstormed... I know, I'll write about planting our vegetable seeds." She then invited the children to suggest details she could add about that activity. The finished letter, like the brainstormed list of topics, was posted on the wall.

Explain the activity clearly to parents

At the launch of the project, Sue sent parents a letter explaining how the journaling would work and the importance of parents writing back to the children every week.

She also gave parents some suggestions on how to respond. For example, she suggested that they write about the same topic as their child, that they print, and that they use the same letter-writing conventions for the date, salutation, and signature that the children used. She also suggested that they have the child read the response with them before bringing the notebooks back on Monday.

Let parents know that the children may be sharing their responses with the class

This helps parents decide what might and might not be appropriate to write. In addition, Sue scanned every notebook before children shared it with classmates.

Give children and families a letter-writing checklist

In Sue's class, each child had a copy of a simple checklist of things to remember when writing a letter—the date, the salutation, the signature, the use of complete sentences, and so forth. Each child attached the checklist to the inside cover of the notebook, where it could serve as a reminder to both the children and their parents.

Build in time for writing and sharing letters

Sue usually set aside time for the children to write their letters on Thursdays. By then, most of the week had passed, so the children had plenty they could write about. Doing the writing on Thursdays also allowed children to take some time on Fridays to finish up if they needed to.

As for sharing the letters with classmates, the students who were scheduled to share at Morning Meeting could choose to read their letters then. In addition, a few students could read their letters during a brief period set aside for that purpose every day after lunch. No student, therefore, had to wait too long to share a letter.

(On the following page is a sample letter to parents about weekend family message journals.)

**Chapter
Four**

Sample Letter to Parents about
Weekend Family Message Journals

Spotlight: Weekend Family Message Journals

[Date]

Dear Parents,

The children and I have a great new project to share with you: the Weekend Family Message Journal. Each Friday, your child will bring home a letter s/he wrote to you, telling one thing about that week at school. Please read each week's message and ask your child to tell you about the message and any accompanying drawing. Don't worry if the message is difficult to read—it's written in primary-level spelling. Your child's messages will become easier to read as the year progresses.

Please write a message back to your child each week in the notebook right after your child's message. Anyone at home is welcome to write back—a parent, a sibling or another relative, or a family friend. The important thing is that your child receives a reply.

To keep this project working smoothly, please:

- Write about the same topic as your child.

- Use print.

- Use a conventional letter-writing format. This letter is an example (date at the top, a greeting on the left, the message below that, and a closing).

- Have your child read your message over with you.

- Send the notebook back with your child each Monday. Your child will have the option of sharing your reply with the class.

The at-home part of this project should take no more than ten to fifteen minutes each week. This short routine, done each week, can be tremendously helpful to your child's learning. Thank you for partnering with your child in this important work!

Please let me know if you have any questions.

Sincerely,

[Teacher's name]

Spotlight:

Reaching Out to Parents in a Low-Income Community

Fifth Grade
Duval Elementary School and
Archer Community School
Gainesville Area, Florida

Ninety-five percent of students at Duval Elementary School in Gainesville, Florida, receive free or reduced-price lunches. At nearby Archer Community School, the figure is seventy percent. In communities with such widespread poverty, many of the basics of teacher-parent contact that are taken for granted in more affluent communities simply aren't available, says fifth grade teacher Sharon Ketts.

Time—to volunteer, to come to school for evening events, even to stop in for a twenty-minute conference—is one thing that is often not available. "Most of these parents are working two or three jobs just to put food on the table. They don't have time for anything else," says Sharon, who taught for many years at Duval before recently moving to Archer.

Even if some parents somehow find the time to come to school, lack of transportation often remains a problem. It's rare for Duval or Archer families to have a car, and in the case of Archer, most of the students live in the area's two housing projects, both of which are far from the school.

The phone isn't a reliable means to keep in touch either. "Most families have frequent disconnects because of nonpayment of bills," Sharon explains. "If they have a cell phone, it's for emergency 9-1-1 use only, or they have a small number of minutes and they've run out of them."

Nonetheless, against such odds, teachers at both schools have persisted and have had successes in communicating with families. Sharon's experience at Archer and Duval has taught her that there's no trick to doing this. It just takes using lots of ways to reach out, and simply keeping at it, she says. "Get creative. Think outside the box. Ask other teachers what's worked for them. Don't rely on any one way. If one way doesn't get a big response, don't give up. Add other methods."

Here are some approaches that Sharon and her colleagues have used:

Daily student binders

Each semester, with Title I money, the school buys a staple-bound booklet for every fourth and fifth grader. The booklet goes into a blue binder where students keep all their schoolwork. It has a section for every curriculum subject area, a section for papers that parents are asked to sign, and a section for homework papers.

Every day on an overhead projector, Sharon shows a replica of a page in the staple-bound booklet and writes on it the day's homework assignment along with notes and reminders to parents. The students copy the information in their own booklets. If Sharon needs to communicate something with a particular parent, she writes a note in that child's booklet. The students take their binders home, where their parents read the booklet, look at the schoolwork in the subject areas, and sign any papers that need to be signed. Parents can also write a note back to the teacher in the booklet if they want to. The next day the students bring the binders back to school.

Spotlight:
Reaching Out
to Parents
in a Low-
Income
Community

In addition, once a week the principal writes a newsletter that's hole-punched and added to the binders. Besides the usual school sharings, the newsletter includes community news that may be of interest to families—homework help available at the church, discounts at the skate park, events at the library. This not only draws families to read the newsletter, but offers them an additional practical service.

Over time, the binder becomes a fairly reliable method of communication because parents come to expect it, says Sharon.

Making school events more convenient for all

To make it easier for parents with varying work schedules to come to conferences, Sharon and colleagues make themselves available as early as 7:00 A.M. and as late as 8:00 P.M., including the evening before the scheduled conference day if necessary. Although attendance is still not high, the flexible meeting times do help get a few more parents in, and that makes the practice worth continuing, says Sharon.

At Duval Elementary, there was also a school-home liaison, employed using Title I money. The liaison helped coordinate family involvement efforts, including picking families up at home to attend school functions if necessary. The liaison program was effective, says Sharon, because the liaison was a community member whom families knew and trusted.

Going to where the families are

Rather than always asking parents to come to school, Sharon often goes to community events where families are likely to be present so she can "just say hello." For example, she sometimes goes to children's community baseball games. Once she went to see some children from the school sing at a local tree lighting ceremony because she knew some of their families would be there. She doesn't talk to the parents about school on these occasions. She just introduces herself as their children's teacher and enjoys the event with the families. The point, she says, is to lay the foundation for a friendly, constructive relationship with them. This less institutionalized, community-oriented way of making contact is something that many parents long for. "It helps teachers understand the family better and how the child lives," says one mother.

Chapter Four

Chapter Five

INVITING PARENTS INTO THE CLASSROOM

*M*y son's teacher welcomes me
into the classroom, announced or unannounced. Her attitude is 'Hey, parent,
whenever you feel you want to come, you can come. I have your kid
for the day, but you're ultimately the parent.'"

Parent of a fourth grader

One time-tested way of involving parents in their children's education is to welcome them to come into the classroom. Other chapters of this book talk about informing parents about classroom life through newsletters, notes, phone calls, postcards, back-to-school nights, and other meetings. In addition to those critical pieces of parent involvement, there's simply opening the doors of the classroom and inviting parents to come observe, take part in, or help out.

An obvious benefit of doing this is that it helps parents better understand how their child is being taught. It's one thing to read and hear about classroom life; it can be quite another to experience it. Often all the explanations about what the children are doing in school and why they're doing it come alive and make more sense when parents are there to see, hear, and feel classroom life for themselves.

But there's another important reason to have parents in the classroom: to enrich children's learning. Parents' presence can add energy and inspiration. They can share their ideas, interests, family traditions, and cultures in person, thereby deepening children's understanding of their classmates and broadening their perspectives on their community and the world. Moreover, teachers can then shape lessons and projects around families' interests and traditions, so that classroom learning and home life feel more connected and integrated for the children.

Yet the majority of parents tend to stay away from school, coming only for the traditional open house or twice-yearly conferences. There are a variety of possible reasons: Perhaps the parents can't get away from work, they're busy, they don't believe a parent's place is in school, they've had a history of negative contacts with school, or they're uncomfortable with the English language. Making matters worse—or at least not helping—is the fact that we teachers sometimes are less than fully welcoming of parents at school. Perhaps we worry that parents won't do or say the right thing when they're working with the children. Or we fear that they'll question or judge how we run our classrooms. Or we simply don't know how to include parents in the activities, and the whole idea of managing a roomful of children and their parents is just too overwhelming. When I first started teaching, I had all these worries and more.

Parents' Roles in the Classroom

In the ensuing years, I learned that I didn't need to do or manage as much as I thought to have parents in the classroom. Most parents just wanted to see what their children were doing in school, so I didn't need to create things for parents to do. For parents who wanted to help out more actively, the coordinating work was manageable. And yes, some parents may say or do things that work against what we're trying to teach students. But careful planning and preparation for parent visits go a long way toward minimizing these discrepancies. Ultimately, the benefits of having parents visit far outweigh any potential drawbacks.

This chapter will discuss some different roles that parents can play in the classroom, then offer some guidelines for successful parent visits.

Parents' Roles in the Classroom

Parents can assume a variety of roles in the classroom and ideally should be able to choose among roles so that their time in the room is comfortable for them and everyone else. Here are some roles that parents can have:

Observer

For many parents, this is the most comfortable role to start with. It involves little risk on their part, but still allows them to experience what's going on in the classroom. Parents might observe one or more parts of the school day: Morning Meeting, reading or writing workshop, science block, math time, social studies, recess, an Academic Choice lesson, and so forth. It depends on what parents want to see and which times fit their schedule.

I've found that work sharing is one thing that parents especially like to see. If there's a scheduled time during the day for children to show and talk about some work they've done, this might be a good time for parents to observe. One favorite time in my room, for example, is Author's Chair, when students share their writing.

Closing circle is another popular time for parents to come. This is a fifteen-minute period at the end of the day when the children and I gather to reflect together on our day—what went well, what we worked hard on, and what we might need to improve on. Also during closing circle, children share work that they're proud of. Parents enjoy hearing students' reflections and finding out the kind of work they're doing in class.

An additional way for parents to observe everyday classroom life—one that might work well for parents who can't come to school during regular school hours—is to use open house time. In most traditional open houses, the children put on a special performance for parents. By contrast, in these open houses the children demonstrate some routine aspect of their day. One year my students and I held a Morning Meeting for parents to watch. Another year we demonstrated closing circle. In other years we've shown parents our daily reading and writing workshop and played our favorite math games. My experience is that parents don't miss the special performances because what they want most is to see what real life in their child's classroom is like.

Participant

As participants, parents join in to do classroom activities alongside the children. For example, third grade teacher Caltha Crowe invites parents to drop in on Wednesdays, any time of the day, to take part in the day's activities. "They're not there to be helpers or passive observers," she says. "They aren't there to see a show or to be the show." Rather, she explains, the purpose of these visits, which she calls Wonderful Wednesdays, is for parents to experience realistic day-to-day classroom life in a safe and relaxed way. (To read more about Wonderful Wednesdays, see Appendix B.)

Some parents come to participate in class for fifteen minutes—perhaps to join in on Morning Meeting—and some come for two hours to experience writers' workshop and math time. Regardless, participating alongside the children often gives parents a deeper understanding of the purpose and value of classroom activities than they can gain from observing the activities.

Sharer

Parents can also come into the classroom to share a hobby, a skill, a cultural tradition, or a family interest. During a unit on ecosystems in one class, a student's father came to show the snakes he collects. That got students interested in learning about the habitats of different kinds of snakes. In another class, a parent came to teach the students how to do simple sewing. The students were able to use what they learned to make costumes for a play they were creating for a social studies project. In yet another classroom, a few parents who spoke a language other than English came at different times during the year to teach the children how to greet one another in different languages; the children could then use those greetings in Morning Meeting. Many teachers invite parents to come tell the children what school was like for them. Parents might come tell about what they do for a living, something that can help children link their classroom learning to the bigger world. Or parents can share a slice of their family culture, which opens children's eyes to the diversity of traditions and lifestyles in their community.

**Parents'
Roles in the
Classroom**

No matter what their interests, what they do for a living, what cultural background they have, and what their family structure, all parents have something valuable to share with the class.

(For an example of how to integrate families' interests into classroom learning, see page 110.)

Helper

For most teachers, there simply are not enough hours in a day to do all they need to do. Parents can offer a very helpful extra pair of hands, and most are eager to do so if they can.

Parents can help in lots of ways. They can do clerical tasks, such as copying or filing papers, hanging up children's work, laminating, or cutting things out. They can also work with individual children, work with small groups, or help with special class projects, which all allow more individualized and small group work in the classroom.

I saw a beautiful example of parents pitching in one morning in Barbara Klein's kindergarten class in Bridgeport, Connecticut. The children were doing a unit on eggs. While the instructional assistant helped children at one table diagram parts of an egg, at another table a parent was helping children weigh eggs using a balance. A short distance away, another parent supervised a group of children making clay models of animals that lay eggs. In another corner, a third parent was playing a Humpty Dumpty board game with a small group of children.

Barbara herself roamed the room overseeing the setup, giving a piece of guidance here, a word of encouragement there. After a period, the children switched locations to try a new activity. The richness and diversity in learning that took place that morning would not have been possible without the parents' help.

Guidelines for Successful Visits

Some careful planning and preparation can make parents' visits to the classroom go more smoothly. Here are some guidelines:

Invite parents often

While it may seem obvious, it's worth emphasizing that to help parents feel sure that they are welcome in the classroom, we may need to invite them often. At the very beginning of the year, I let parents know that I welcome each of them to come share a hobby, interest, or family tradition sometime during the year. At back-to-school night I ask parents if they'd like to come help out with various jobs in the classroom. Throughout the year I repeat these general invitations as well as inviting parents for specific activities and events.

Chapter Five

Whether for specific events or general visiting, I often have the students create written invitations. The children enjoy doing this, and it gives them practice in literacy skills. In addition, I've found that parents are more likely to come when the invitation is from their child.

Find out how parents would like to be involved

Anytime during the year, when parents have an idea for something they would like to share with the class or something they would like to help out with, they should be able to approach the teacher. However, for planning purposes, it helps if the teacher gets a sense early in the year of what parents might be interested in. Here are two ways to gather this information:

Family interest inventory early in the year

During the first weeks of school, I send parents a family interest inventory, asking them to list any special interests, skills, talents, or family traditions that they would be willing to share with the class. As I plan the curriculum over the course of the year, I try to incorporate these offerings as much as possible. (See Chapter 2 for more on family interest inventories.)

Helpers' signup sheet at back-to-school night

At back-to-school night, I mention to parents my interest in having volunteers help out in the classroom during the year. I explain briefly the different ways parents can help, then refer parents to the clipboard at the back table where they can see a detailed list of jobs. Parents interested in helping can then write down their name, check off the work they're willing to do, indicate how often they'd like to help, and which days and times work best for them.

With this information I create a master calendar of volunteers for the year. I try to give each volunteer the same day every week or month so I don't have to keep setting up appointments. I keep a separate list of parents who can only help occasionally during the year and call these parents whenever the class has a special project for which we need an extra pair of hands.

Guidelines for Successful Visits

Emphasize that *all* parents have something valuable to share

Sometimes parents feel like they have nothing of value to share with the class. For example, some feel that if they didn't go to college and don't have a prestigious or glamorous job, they don't have anything the children would find interesting. Third grade teacher Ramona McCullough in Chantilly, Virginia, was able to cut through that misconception when she organized a career day one year. She invited *all* parents to come talk about what they do for a living, emphasizing that they each had something to contribute, no matter what their job. The parents who came included a seamstress, a lawyer, a mechanic, a doctor, a plumber, a home day care provider, a bus driver, a politician, a writer, an assembly line worker, a grocery store clerk, a police officer, a custodian, a teacher, and a nurse. Ramona made them all feel significant, and the children learned from each of them.

Similarly, when teachers invite parents to tell something about their home culture, some parents—particularly White Americans whose families have been in this country for generations—may feel that while new immigrants might have interesting customs to share, they themselves are just "plain old Americans" and don't have any "culture" that others would find interesting. "But I try to tell parents that all Americans are not the same," says K–1 teacher Margaret Sullivan, who invites every parent to give a brief sharing about some family tradition or interest during the year. "In one family, the grandmother might live with them and be a big part of their lives. That's not true for all families," says the New

London, Connecticut, teacher. In another family, monthly extended family meals followed by card games may be a tradition. In yet another family, trips to the beach with neighbors may be an annual occurrence. As teachers, we can reassure parents that the children are fascinated by all these traditions, and that even sharings that may seem mundane can spark or powerfully reinforce classroom lessons.

Decide how often to have drop-in visits

Many teachers welcome parents to drop in to the classroom anytime, announced or unannounced. Other teachers specify certain days and times for drop-ins. Each teacher should decide what's best for her/him, the parents, and the students. One teacher may decide that Tuesdays are best for parent visits because the children don't have specials that day. Another may decide it would be best for parents to come during Morning Meetings, Academic Choice lessons, or writers' workshops so they can see those kinds of learning approaches.

Parents may be more apt to drop in if teachers provide them with a schedule of activities. For example, when Caltha Crowe invites parents to Wonderful Wednesdays, she includes the day's schedule in the invitation, and she sticks to that schedule every Wednesday. That way, parents can plan to come experience the subject or activity that they're most interested in.

Be clear what the parent's role will be

Classroom visits are most successful when both the teacher and the parent are clear on what the parent's role is—observer, participant, sharer, or helper. It's often best to state the role for the particular visit explicitly when making arrangements. For example, in Caltha's Wonderful Wednesdays invitation, she writes, "Join us as frequently or as infrequently as you please. All we ask is that you join us as a participant in our activities." (See Appendix B for details.)

Provide written guidelines for visitors

I've found it's a good idea to send parents some written guidelines for classroom visits. The guidelines explain the general goals I have for children's learning and offer some tips on how parents can help. Here's a sample:

**Guidelines
for Successful
Visits**

[Date]

Dear Parents,

The children and I welcome you to visit our classroom throughout the year. Whether you come to observe, share something, take part in classroom activities, or help out, we look forward to having you.

Our goal in this classroom is for children to be independent workers who support one another by working cooperatively and with self-control. To encourage this, and to help ensure that your visit is a positive experience for everyone, please keep these tips in mind:

- During independent work times, feel free to interact with children by asking them to tell you about their work or what they're doing.

- If you're observing a lesson, focus on what the children are doing. If you have any questions to ask me, please save them until after I've finished working with the children.

- Interact with all children in addition to your own child.

- Give help only when a child asks for it. Start by asking the child what s/he has already tried.

- Please follow the rules of our classroom, particularly the signals we use. A rung bell or a raised hand means "Freeze. Quiet. Listen."

Thank you very much!

Sincerely,

[Teacher's name]

Consider a "first-time helpers" meeting

For parents who volunteer to work with children in the classroom, a "first-time helpers" meeting can be useful. At the meeting, the teacher can offer some general tips on working with children. For example, the teacher can:

Remind helpers to let children do their own work

The helper's role is to observe, support, and encourage the children.

Give models for conversation with children

For example:

- To reinforce positive behavior, the helper can say, "I notice that you are cooperating with your partner" or "I see that you did all the problems."

- To help a child but not do the child's work for him/her, the helper can say, "Tell me some of the ways you've already tried" or "How can I help you figure this problem out?"

- To reflect with a child on work done, the helper can say, "Tell me about your drawing" or "What's your favorite part of your picture?"

Teach parents the classroom signal for attention

For example:

- Ringing a bell

- Raising a hand

Make sure parents feel free to call upon the teacher

They may need to do this, for example, when a simple reminder or redirection doesn't improve problematic behavior.

Give parents needed reminders privately

Even when parents are clear on their role during a visit, have been given visitors' guidelines, and have attended a first-time helpers' meeting, they may not always speak or act in the classroom as we might wish them to. Everyone forgets and makes mistakes sometimes. I've sometimes had to remind parents to focus on all the children, not just their own, or to let children work on a problem before rushing in with a solution, or to follow our classroom signal for quiet. The important thing is to hold such conversations privately, never in front of the children, and to use a respectful and empathic tone. It can help to connect the reminder with what we're trying to teach the children. For example, I might say, "I know it's hard to watch a child struggle with a tough math concept. I have to remind myself that they actually learn more and become more independent, and feel better about themselves, when they struggle and figure it out."

When Parents Can't Come to School

For a variety of reasons—work schedules, transportation problems, illness, lack of child care—some parents simply cannot come to school. Teachers can involve these parents in classroom life in other ways. Here are just two ideas:

When Parents Can't Come to School

Videotaping classroom activities

In my classroom, I have a video camera set up in one corner. Whenever the children are doing something I know their parents would be interested in, or when we have a special event, I turn the camera on. I make a few copies of the tape and send it home with children to watch with their parents. It's not the same as being there, but at least the parents have a view of their child in action during the school day.

In the book *Together is Better: Collaborative Assessment, Evaluation & Reporting,* the authors suggest gluing a simple form to the video box. On the form, the teacher writes what the class is doing in the video and the key elements s/he would like parents to notice. There's also a space on the form for each parent borrowing the tape to write a brief comment. (Davies et. al. 1992, 51)

A panel of "email experts"

In the book *Conversations: Strategies for Teaching, Learning, and Evaluating* by Regie Routman, teacher Lee Sattelmeyer talks about using email to involve families in classroom life. Lee asked parents at the beginning of the year whether they had access to email, what expertise they had through their jobs, hobbies, or interests, and whether they would be willing to volunteer to answer students' questions about their various areas of expertise via email. Lee then created a list of "email experts" for the students to consult when questions surfaced during their learning. The students would email a parent who was likely to be able to help find the answers. Many times, too, the "email expert" would initiate an exchange by sending a question for the students to investigate. It was a great way for parents to be part of classroom life from a distance. In addition, it gave students an opportunity to work with computers and to practice communicating their ideas clearly through writing. (Routman 2000, 513-514)

(For another example of involving parents who can't come to the classroom, see "Parent Publishing Group" on page 113.)

A Richness That Teachers Alone Cannot Provide

Though creating structures for involving parents in classroom life requires an initial investment of time and energy, these structures mostly sustain themselves. There are significant benefits to such involvement. It can be powerful for children to see their parents as respected and visible participants in school life. The regular presence of students' parents in the classroom can also bring a diversity of style and a richness of experience that no teacher alone can provide.

Chapter Five

Spotlight:

Building Families' Interests into the Curriculum

Primary grades
Heath Elementary School
Heath, Massachusetts

Spotlight:
Building
Families'
Interests
into the
Curriculum

Having parents help out with classroom activities is great. The students, the parents, and the teacher all benefit. Heath, Massachusetts, teacher Deborah Porter has taken this a step further, however. Instead of simply having parents help with a curriculum that's already in place, she builds families' interests into the curriculum itself.

A recent weaving project is an example. Learning about patterns is one of the first things children do in math in Deborah's class. "We create patterns with our bodies, we sing them, build them, clap them," says the longtime primary teacher. "But I never realized the true possibilities in studying patterns until one student gave me a small, beautiful weaving."

The student, David, made the weaving himself with help from his mom. Her curiosity piqued, Deborah talked to David's mom and discovered that weaving was a hobby of hers. When the parent volunteered to teach the whole class to weave, Deborah immediately said yes.

What ensued was a long project on weaving that brought all the children's understanding of patterns to life. The children brought cloth from home and, with the parent's help, worked together to weave the strips into a larger work. They compared strips, studied colors, traded cloth, and planned how they wanted their pattern to go. As they helped each other work the loom, fixing missed warps and making sure the weaving was tight enough to hold, the study of patterns took on a whole new meaning and level of interest.

Spanning several areas of learning

As the children wove, they developed an eye for patterns all around them. The project therefore quickly grew past the boundaries of math, spilling into other subject areas. The children saw patterns in everything, from the poetry they read to the animals they studied.

"When I choose projects that consciously connect children's home life and school life, our classroom work becomes broader and more interesting than anything I could offer myself," says Deborah.

Bringing in families' interests doesn't mean squeezing out required content either. "In fact, the beauty of projects is that it's nearly impossible for them not to cover multiple content areas," Deborah notes. She still teaches the same subjects and skills; she just teaches them in a way that integrates the families' interests.

Connecting learning to children's home lives

Beyond making learning come alive and integrating different content areas, there's a more fundamental reason to build families' interests into the curriculum.

"Remember the story of the blind men and the elephant?" Deborah asks. The story goes that each of six blind men feels a different part of an elephant and then is certain that he knows what an elephant is just from the part he felt. As the men argue over who is right, they get further and further from the truth.

"Expecting students to learn a subject in isolation from the context of their home and community life is like expecting them to know what an elephant is from feeling one floppy ear," explains Deborah. Subjects and skills make more sense and have greater meaning for children when they're connected to the stuff of their daily lives. By opening up the curriculum to let family interests in, teachers are doing nothing more or less than their job: allowing children to learn at their best.

Tips for teachers who want to use this approach

Get to know parents from the beginning of the year

Ask parents what goals they have for their child this year. While letting them know something about your approach to teaching, invite them to share any information that would help you work better with their child. These beginnings can naturally lead to ongoing conversations about the families' interests, hobbies, and traditions. Many teachers send written questionnaires asking parents to describe their interests. (See Chapter 2 for more on beginning-of-the-year activities with parents.)

Stay alert to family interests throughout the year

Informal conversations with parents, objects that students bring to school, and things children say in sharings are all clues.

Extend an invitation

Once you see how a family's interest can fit into the curriculum, invite the parent to share it with the class. Don't wait for parents to volunteer. They may not see how their interests can help the class. Or they may think that if you don't ask for their involvement, you must not want it.

Let parents know clearly what their role is

In projects like these, the parent should be the content specialist. For example, the parent who taught weaving helped the children get started on their project, then checked in every few days to see how they were coming along. Parents should not take on the role of managing the class or even of being in charge of a lesson. These must remain the teacher's job if the class is to function smoothly. Being clear on roles can also relieve parents of anxiety about taking part, says Deborah: "When I say, 'You don't have to manage the class. Just show us the weaving,' they're more likely to say, 'Oh, okay, I can do that.'"

Spotlight: Building Families' Interests into the Curriculum

Plan few projects

Just one or two a year will go a long way. Although only one parent may be involved at the outset of a project, other parents often get drawn in along the way. Teachers often note, too, that children often feel the school-home connection even when it's not their own parent who's in the classroom.

Work with state frameworks

"Rather than seeing state frameworks as a burden, I try to see them as a guide in making sure the class is learning all they need to be learning," says Deborah. As teachers get to know the frameworks better, it should become easier to see which requirements are being met by the project work, she says. To help with the assessment and documentation of children's progress in these required areas, Deborah posts the frameworks inside her closet door for easy reference and keeps a notebook, tape recorder, and camera handy for recording children at work.

Spotlight:

Parent Publishing Group

Third Grade
Frederick Harris School
Springfield, Massachusetts

For many parents, physically getting in to their children's classroom can be an impossible luxury. Any number of reasons—work, lack of transportation, having to take care of other family members—can stand in the way and leave these parents feeling distant from school life. At Frederick Harris School in Springfield, Massachusetts, David Cirone's third grade class has a solution: a parent publishing group that gives parents a meaningful way to be involved in classroom life without physically being present.

David and room parent Allison McCann enlist a handful of parents to be a "publisher" of students' writing. Using cardboard, construction paper, and other common materials, the parents make a supply of blank books. Once a quarter, every student submits a piece of writing for publication—any poetry, fiction, or essay the student is proud of. The parents then type up the pieces on their own time in their own homes. The typed pages are returned a couple of weeks later to the classroom, where each student glues his/her typed work onto the pages of a blank book, then adds illustrations.

By the end of the year, every student will have published four books. All these student-created books live in the classroom library. Throughout the year, classmates can read each other's books and write comments on the blank pages that are included at the end of each volume.

Based on an idea in language arts teacher Regie Routman's book *Invitations: Changing as Teachers and Learners K–12,* the publishing project works because publishing is such a powerful motivator for children. "Students like seeing their work printed out and put in book form," David explains. "They like having other kids read their books. They work harder on the writing when they know it has to be clear enough for a parent—their own or another's—to read and type up. It all makes them feel like a real author."

For parents in the publishing group, the prime benefit is knowing what their children are doing in the classroom. "They miss that," says Allison of parents who can't get to school. "They can see 'Oh, they're doing poetry' or 'They're up to five-paragraph essays,'" adds David. Allison says the parents also simply enjoy reading the stories the children write. "They learn a lot about their child from the stories: not only what they're working on in school, but what they're thinking about and who their friends are."

For the busy teacher with too much to do, having a parent publishing group means having some much needed help. With parents doing the concrete tasks of typing and book construction, the teacher is freed to spend more time on helping students write, revise, edit, and proofread.

Finally, the publishing group can become a way for families to get to know one another. "I long for a sense of community with other parents and with the school," says Allison. "This provides that. I feel involved."

Spotlight:
Parent
Publishing
Group

Tips for starting a parent publishing group

Explain the purpose to parents

Explain that the goal of publishing is to motivate children to write. Many adults want their children to enjoy and get better at writing. Emphasizing this goal may help generate more interest.

Rely on parents to help organize

The parent publishing group in David's class began with two people: himself and room parent Allison McCann. An active networker and a familiar face among the other parents, Allison got more parents to join and then began serving as project coordinator.

Be specific in what help you're asking for

Instead of asking "What can you do to help with this project?", Allison suggests asking, "We need six parents who can each type four 300-word stories a quarter. Can you do that?"

Be reassuring and use lay terms

Parents often feel intimidated by school projects, saying, "I don't spell well" or thinking they can't help if they don't have an advanced degree, says Allison. Reassure them that they are only being asked to type and aren't expected to correct or edit the writing. Let them know their help is valuable. Using lay terms when talking and in written notices is also important, Allison says.

Keep it cheap

Beautiful books can be made out of ordinary cardboard, construction paper, glue, and fasteners. Many teachers collect discontinued wallpaper samples from local wallpaper stores to use in decorating book covers.

Provide detailed bookmaking steps along with a constructed sample

To ensure that the books will all be of the same high quality, spell out how big the book should be, how to affix the wallpaper, and how to bind the pages. (David and Allison adapt guidelines from Routman's book *Invitations*.) Also specify the margins, font, type size, and line spacing to use when typing the students' writing. (See sample on the next page.)

Be clear about correcting children's writing

Although students should submit final, polished writing for publication, occasional spelling or grammar mistakes get through. Be clear whether you want parents to correct mistakes they notice. To preserve students' voices, David tells parents not to change anything beyond basic spelling and grammar.

Start small

Start by publishing no more than one piece of writing per student each quarter. Or publish less frequently. This ensures that all the book construction and typing can get done in a timely manner. Expand the project when more parents sign on to help and the process is flowing smoothly.

Chapter Five

**Sample Parent Guidelines
for Typing the Children's Books**

**Spotlight:
Parent
Publishing
Group**

Parent Publishing Project

Thank you so much for volunteering your time to type stories by students in Mr. Cirone's class. Enclosed you will find a student's story. Below are instructions for typing it. I have also attached a sample page from a student's story as an example.

- Set the left margin at 1 inch, the right at 4.6 inches.

- Type the story in 14 or 16 point font.

- Double space the lines.

- The stories have gone through the writing process, so you can just type them as is. If you want, you may correct small punctuation mistakes and spelling errors.

- Feel free to be creative in using different and/or larger fonts for the title and author's name.

- Print the story onto white paper. (If you cannot do that, save the story onto the disc provided and send the disc back to school. We will print it. Please save the document in Word.)

- Send the story back to school with your child for delivery to Mr. Cirone.

Thanks again for helping with this great literacy project. We would love to show you the finished products. If you have any questions, please feel free to contact me.

Allison McCann

Room Parent

The Experiment

The Experiment!!!

By
Charles Goodine

Chapter Five

The first few pages of one third grader's book, published by the class's parent publishing group.

Dr. Smith had just finished building a rocket that would go to Pluto. He wiped his hands and said, "just another day at work". Then, Dr. Cirone came rushing to the door. Out of breathe, he said, "doc…doctor…Smi…Smith. Let me catch my breath. We need to build another rocket for charity by Christmas Eve, so we can have it ready for Christmas day". "But it's already December first", said Dr. Smith.

"I've already been to every planet, and all of the rockets were very durable", said Dr. Smith. "Well", said Dr. Cirone, "you have to make a brand new one". "Ok, we need to think, think, think about this", said Dr. Smith. "Oh!!! I've got it", yelled Dr. Cirone. "We need to get back to the lab as soon as possible". Soon, they were in the car and on their way to the lab in Vermont. It was a long ride from Tennessee.

While they were driving, Dr. Cirone explained his plan to build a rocket out of the old house on Maple St., so they went straight to Maple St. As soon as they got there, they got together their supplies and got right to work. "Hammer, screwdriver, saw,

Chapter Six

SHARING INFORMATION ABOUT CLASSROOM PRACTICES

M*y son's school recently started using a new approach to math. It was something I didn't learn when I was in school, and I couldn't help him with his work. I told the teacher, "I don't know how to do this." A lot of other parents said the same thing, so the school held a math night to introduce the approach to parents.*

Parent of a fourth grader

In today's education environment, where the teaching of social and academic skills is often very different from what parents experienced when they were in school, it's perhaps more important than ever for teachers to help parents understand their classroom practices. In addition to the ongoing communication discussed in Chapter 4, there are times when parents would benefit from an explanation about specific classroom practices, be it the teacher's approach to discipline or a new math program the children are using.

Parents need information about the expectations, curricula, strategies, and activities in their children's classroom. They need to know not only what their children are doing, but why and how. Once parents know the what, why, and how, they can be more supportive of their children's learning.

Few teachers, of course, would argue that parents should be kept in the dark. But when we get busy with all the demands of teaching, we sometimes forget to share information with parents. One year when I was teaching fourth grade, our school district adopted a new math curriculum. It consisted of statistics, probability, geometry, algebra, and more. I couldn't believe what a nine-year-old was expected to learn. I soon discovered that this math curriculum reflected what was on the fourth grade state proficiency test. I didn't agree with the new curriculum or the new state tests, but I knew I had to plunge forward and begin preparing my students. Perhaps it was because I was wrapped up in my own frustration that I didn't think to explain the math curriculum to parents.

One day, during our algebra unit, I assigned some equations for the children to practice for homework. My phone rang off the hook that night. Frustrated, confused parents complained that they didn't know how to help their children solve the equations and they didn't see why a fourth grader should be expected to do algebra in the first place.

The next day I wrote a letter of apology, explaining the new curriculum and its connection to the state tests. Once the parents understood what the school was doing and why, they became more supportive.

Goals in Explaining Classroom Practices

I certainly learned my lesson about adequately informing parents of classroom practices through this incident. I learned about the frustration and anger that can result when parents don't understand the rationale behind what we do, and I saw the support and collaboration they can offer when they do understand. As teachers, we can take steps to encourage the latter to happen.

Goals in Explaining Classroom Practices

These are the main goals in helping parents understand our classroom practices:

To enable parents to take an active role in their children's school life

When parents understand the classroom curriculum, they're more able to help with schoolwork, hold meaningful conversations with their child about school, and offer helpful feedback to the teacher.

To help parents trust that their child is getting a good education

While some parents will implicitly trust that the teacher is doing a good job educating their children, we cannot expect all parents to have that feeling automatically. We can encourage that trust, however, by informing them of what we're teaching, and the hows and whys behind it.

To harness the full power of our best practices

When we explain our teaching to parents, we make it possible for them to reinforce at home the expectations and lessons of the classroom. We gain a valuable partner in educating the child, and we show the child that their parents and teacher are on the same team.

Helping Parents Understand the *Responsive Classroom* Approach

I use the *Responsive Classroom* approach to teaching. Used by teachers and schools around the country for over twenty years, it consists of practical strategies for integrating social and academic learning throughout the school day. It infuses all aspects of my teaching, from guiding the language I use with students to influencing how I set up the physical classroom. Many of the practices I discuss in this chapter are part of the *Responsive Classroom* approach. It's therefore one of the first things I help parents understand. Early in the school year, and sometimes even before the first day of school, I send parents a letter that gives an overview of this approach. (For a sample letter, see Appendix C.)

Throughout the year, as I introduce individual components of the approach into our classroom life, I provide separate, more detailed explanations of those specific components. (See samples throughout this chapter.)

Chapter Six

Over the years I've found there are certain classroom practices that are especially important for parents to understand. In this chapter, I'll talk about those and share some ideas for communicating about them.

Approach to Classroom Discipline

One of the most important topics to talk with parents about is our approach to discipline in the classroom. The more information we can provide about this, and the earlier in the year we can begin providing it, the better.

A letter during the first weeks of school

Many teachers send home a letter early in the year explaining the classroom rules. In my classroom, the students help create the rules by first articulating their hopes and dreams for the year, and then thinking about what rules we'll need in order to allow everyone to make his/her hopes and dreams come true. Early in the year I send parents a letter explaining this process.

This letter also gives information on logical consequences for rule breaking. Because some families may assume that logical consequences are the same as punishments, it's important to help them see the difference. I find that it helps to describe briefly the three types of logical consequences I use and give some examples of each. Also, as is true when explaining any classroom practice, it's as important to explain the intentions behind using logical consequences as it is to explain the practice itself.

A sample letter is shown below.

(To learn more about this approach to discipline, see *Rules in School* by Kathryn Brady, Mary Beth Forton, Deborah Porter, and Chip Wood, published by Northeast Foundation for Children, 2003.)

Approach to Classroom Discipline

[Date]

Dear Parents,

The children and I have been talking a lot during these first weeks of school about our hopes and dreams for the year and about our classroom rules. Each child thought about his/her hopes and dreams and shared them with the class. (You may want to ask your child about this.) Then the class figured out the kinds of rules we'll need if all of us are to reach our hopes and dreams. Here are the rules we came up with:

- Be in control of yourself.

- Be respectful of everyone.

- Take care of our classroom and school.

- Always try your best.

We recognize that no one can be expected to follow the rules 100% of the time. When children make mistakes in following the rules, I'll help them solve the problems caused by their mistakes through the use of "logical consequences." Logical consequences are not punishments. They are ways to help children see the effects of their actions, repair the situation, and learn to do better next time.

There are three kinds of logical consequences:

Time-out: If a child is being disruptive, s/he goes to a designated spot in the room to pull back together. The time-out is short. The child comes

Discussing the topic again at back-to-school night

It is not enough just to send parents a letter about our discipline approach at the beginning of the year. Parents need to hear about this topic throughout the year in different ways. I find back-to-school night to be a great time to come back to this topic. Talking about discipline face-to-face has some important advantages: It allows me to elaborate on some details, and it allows parents to ask questions immediately.

---

back as soon as s/he has regained control. Children may go voluntarily to time-out.

Loss of privilege: If a child misuses a material or acts out during an activity, that child will be told to stop using the material or stop doing the activity for a short period of time. The privilege will be restored when the child and teacher have talked about how to prevent a similar problem in the future.

"You break it, you fix it": If a child damages something or hurts someone's feelings, s/he will try to fix the damage. In the case of hurting someone's feelings, the child might offer an "apology of action" by writing a card, helping with an activity, making an illustration, or taking some other action beyond verbally saying "sorry."

My goal is to help children believe in their ability to create a caring learning environment. Learning to live by the rules they've created is an important step.

Please feel free to call me if you have any questions or comments. Thank you.

Sincerely,

[Teacher's name]

Chapter Six

In the discussion, I cover the following:

The goal of my discipline approach

I emphasize that I have two interests in mind when teaching discipline: the interest of each individual child, and the interest of the whole group of children. "The goal is to help each child develop self-discipline while establishing a calm and safe environment for learning," I might say.

"This is not a new approach," I often tell parents. "It's been used during the past twenty years by many teachers using the *Responsive Classroom* approach. It draws on the thinking of many great educators, theorists, and child psychologists."

The rules that the class created

Approach to Classroom Discipline

I remind parents of how our classroom rules came to be and what their purpose is. "The children and I developed these rules together. They came from our desire to make our hopes and dreams for fourth grade come true," I might say. "I've found that students are more motivated to follow rules that they helped to create."

I then point out our displays of the children's hopes and dreams and the class rules. Typically the children will all have signed the rules. I sometimes invite parents to add their signatures. Finally, I encourage families to keep a copy of the rules at home and talk with their child about them throughout the year.

Why the rules are so general

Parents usually notice right away that our class rules are global in nature and few in number. I explain why. "Long lists of rules—no running in the room, no hitting, no pushing, no cutting in line, stay in your seat, raise your hand to talk, don't interrupt—are overwhelming and hard to remember," I might say. A long list of rules also becomes prescriptive, encouraging simple compliance. "By contrast, a short list of global rules encourages children to think on their own about how to apply general expectations to various situations that they find themselves in," I explain.

I let parents know that we spend time discussing, modeling, and practicing how to apply the global rules to different aspects of our school day, so that the children are actively taught how to live by the rules.

Logical consequences for rule breaking

The point I emphasize most about logical consequences is their purpose. "All children will break the rules sometimes. It doesn't mean they're bad. They're testing. It's through testing that children come to understand what the rules really mean," I sometimes say. "In the process of testing, children will make mistakes." The purpose of logical consequences, I continue, is "to help students fix and learn from their mistakes while maintaining a safe and orderly classroom. It's in the spirit of helping children learn from their mistakes, rather than punishing them, that I use logical consequences."

I then briefly repeat the three kinds of logical consequences. Especially in the case of time-out, hearing again about its purpose and how it's used can help parents clear up any misunderstandings about this strategy.

How parents can support classroom discipline

I tell parents that from time to time I may prompt conversations at home about class rules and logical consequences. For example, I give them a heads-up that in my weekly "Ask me about…" newsletter (see Chapter 4), I might include things such as "Ask me about the purpose of time-out" and "Ask me about the Apology of Action chart and how the class uses it."

I also ask parents to support our classroom discipline approach by allowing their child to experience natural consequences whenever possible and safe. For example, if a child forgets to bring her homework to school, I urge them not to rescue the child by bringing it to school. While acknowledging how hard this might be, I point out that the child will learn more if allowed to experience having to re-do the homework. "Don't worry that I'll think you're a bad parent," I say. "I'll think just the opposite. And I'll appreciate your support of our classroom approach to discipline."

Tidbits throughout the year

Throughout the rest of the year, I continue to communicate tidbits about my discipline approach—through "Ask me about…" newsletters, chats during conferences, and brief mentions of the topic in phone calls.

So often, teachers and parents find themselves in opposition when a discipline problem comes up in school. In my experience, the reason often is that parents don't understand the expectations and discipline approach used at school. While it's not the school's place to judge which discipline approach is universally better or to tell parents to conform to the school's approach when disciplining their children at home, I believe it is necessary and helpful for teachers to let parents know that in this classroom, these are the expectations, this is the approach used, and

Chapter Six

here's why. I've found that generally the better informed parents are of classroom discipline practices, the more likelihood of successful teacher-parent collaboration, especially when problems arise.

Unfamiliar Curriculum Approaches and Classroom Activities

In addition to informing parents about our classroom discipline practices, it's important to help them understand any classroom activity or learning approach that they may not be familiar with. Again, I use a combination of methods for this communication, from "Ask me about…" newsletters to formal presentations at back-to-school night.

Here are some of the topics that I take time to explain to parents:

Morning Meeting

Unfamiliar Curriculum Approaches and Classroom Activities

This is a twenty-minute meeting that the children and I have at the beginning of each day. In Morning Meeting, students greet each other, share news, do a group activity, and receive announcements about the day ahead. To introduce parents to this routine for building community and practicing social and academic skills, I send a letter early in the year. A sample is shown on the facing page.

Knowing that some, but certainly not the majority, of the parents will be able to come to our classroom for a Morning Meeting, I look for opportunities to let parents experience it in other gatherings. For example, I begin back-to-school nights with a Morning Meeting modified for adults. (See Chapter 2.)

Academic Choice

Academic Choice is an approach to giving children choices in their learning to help them become invested, self-motivated learners. Within guidelines set by the teacher, the children make choices about what and/or how they will learn. Academic Choice is always carefully designed, with the children choosing activities related to the curriculum and planning what they will do, then reflecting upon what they've accomplished so that they might make improvements next time. However, to someone unfamiliar with Academic Choice, this purposefulness may not be obvious. As K–1 teacher Jeremy Nellis says, "Some parents see chaos instead of every child doing a different planned activity. When I explain Academic Choice, I shine a light on it for them."

A sample letter to parents about Academic Choice can be found on page 128.

(To learn more about Academic Choice, see *Learning Through Academic Choice* by Paula Denton, published by Northeast Foundation for Children, 2005.)

[Date]

Dear Parents:

Our class is busy developing into a caring learning community. We begin each day with Morning Meeting, a twenty-minute gathering during which we practice the academic skills we're working on as well as important social skills such as listening, speaking, problem solving, and group participation.

Morning Meeting has four parts:

- Greeting: Each child is greeted by name and welcomed.

- Sharing: A few children share news and interests, which helps the children get to know each other.

- Group Activity: We might play a cooperation game, recite a poem together, sing a song, or do a math or language activity together.

- Morning Message: The children read a message I've written on big chart paper that helps them look forward to the day ahead.

Morning Meeting is a wonderful part of our day. The children and I would like to invite you to share a Morning Meeting with us. Please let me know, with a few days' notice, when you would like to come take part in a Morning Meeting.

Thank you. The children and I look forward to having you.

Sincerely,

[Teacher's name]

Chapter Six

**Unfamiliar
Curriculum
Approaches
and
Classroom
Activities**

[Date]

Dear Parents,

This year our class will engage in an exciting approach to learning called Academic Choice. Research has shown that when children have some choices about their schoolwork, they are more motivated and engaged, and the quality of their work often improves. Children often say that Academic Choice makes learning more fun.

Here's how Academic Choice works. During some of our lessons, children will be given choices about how they will learn or what they will learn. For example, they might choose among several different ways to practice spelling words or decide which eight vocabulary words they will learn from a list of ten. At other times children will decide how to share what they have learned. For example, to tell about a character in a book we read, they might have the choice of writing a paragraph or report, drawing and captioning illustrations, creating a model, or performing a pantomime.

Academic Choice will always be part of a carefully constructed lesson plan and designed to help your child meet important learning goals. The children will have an opportunity to plan what they will do and I will guide their planning as needed. When their choice work is completed, children will reflect on what they have accomplished and what they would like to improve upon next time. This process helps children become increasingly productive and independent as they make more choices throughout the year.

I look forward to a wonderful year of learning with Academic Choice. Please feel free to contact me if you have any questions.

Sincerely,

[Teacher's name]

Reading, writing, and math approaches

As my fourth grade algebra incident shows, parents are often bewildered by the new ways in which children today are taught core subjects like reading, writing, and math, and they want clarification.

In her book *Conversations,* language arts teacher and workshop presenter Regie Routman offers examples of ways to communicate with parents about how children are learning reading and writing. Over the years I've adapted many of these examples. I've found it helpful to give parents short brochures and letters written in plain, non-jargon language that explains the following:

- How good readers read and how children are taught to read and write in our class

- What reading and writing activities parents can expect to find in their child's classroom

- How children are taught to choose reading books that are right for them

- Strategies children are taught for understanding what they read

- The writing and editing process used in our class

- How students learn to spell in our class

(For examples, see *Conversations* by Regie Routman, published by Heinemann, 2000.)

Teachers can provide parents similar kinds of information about their approach to teaching math. At Six to Six Interdistrict Magnet School in Bridgeport, Connecticut, parents are invited to an evening with a math consultant to hear about the new math approach being used at the school. After the consultant's presentation, parents go to their child's classroom where the classroom teacher explains what the new approach looks like in that particular grade. "Thank goodness we could go to that parent night," says Adair Heitmann, parent of a kindergartner. "When I was a kid, math—in fact, everything—was taught by rote. Now there's much more kinesthetic learning, learning through organized play, lots of right brain and left brain stuff. I would've been totally lost on the new math if it hadn't been for that parent night. It gave us as parents a window into how our kids were being taught."

Upcoming projects

When the class is about to start a unit or project that might be somewhat unusual, it helps to give parents a heads-up, especially if the work might prove a little challenging to students. Similarly, when a change to the schedule or the children's routine is anticipated, it's good to let parents know ahead of time. Having advanced notice gives parents a chance to ask questions and lets them prepare their children and themselves if needed.

Here's a sample letter from Chantilly, Virginia, teacher Ramona McCullough to let parents know of an upcoming biography project:

Unfamiliar Curriculum Approaches and Classroom Activities

[Date]

Dear Parents:

Our class will soon be starting our biography project. Each student will be studying a historical figure and completing a research project. It will consist of three parts:

1. Written report that includes the following:

Paragraph 1: Introduction of historical figure—
birthplace, childhood, education, etc.

Paragraph 2: Important contributions and accomplishments

Paragraph 3: Summary—Why is this person important to you,
our society, our history?

Each paragraph should be three to five well-written, edited sentences. Your child may get information from the school and public library or the Internet. The report should be in your child's own words and in final draft form. It may be typed or neatly handwritten.

2. Oral report—A brief summary of the information in the written report. Note cards may be used as an aid, but I will be asking students not to read from them.

3. Paper doll—Each child will make a paper outline of a person and decorate it to portray accurately the historical figure that s/he researched.

Please contact me if you have any questions about this upcoming project.

Sincerely,

Ramona McCullough

Standardized Tests

Standardized testing is a fact of life in most schools today. Understandably, like many teachers, parents often have a lot of anxiety about testing that they transfer to their children. When children are anxious, it's difficult for them to learn and to do well on the tests.

Regardless of how we ourselves feel about standardized tests, we can help parents feel more relaxed about them by providing adequate information. We can let parents know when testing will take place, what the tests measure, what the results mean for each child, and how parents can best support their child through the testing. Sending home a letter explaining the tests; talking with parents at back-to-school nights, conferences, open houses; and chatting informally before, during, or after school all help to demystify the tests, answer parents' questions, and alleviate their anxiety.

I have also found it helpful to send home a letter the week before the tests to give families some tips on making the testing week a successful one. A sample letter is on page 132.

When Parents Disagree with a Classroom Practice

Just because we are proactive and take the time to help families understand our classroom practices doesn't mean that they will all agree with everything we do or support all our classroom decisions.

I can remember when I first began using Morning Meeting in my fourth grade classroom. After introducing the approach to parents at back-to-school night, I got a letter from Nathan's mom. She was concerned that her son would not be challenged enough and would not be ready to take the fourth grade proficiency test if we spent twenty minutes each day doing a Morning Meeting. I called her after school that day to set up a time to talk in person so I could better understand her concerns. We set up a meeting for the end of the week. I needed time to prepare what I was going to say, and I needed to let some time go by so that I could talk to Nathan's mom without feeling defensive.

When I met with her that Friday, I spent most of the time listening, paraphrasing what she said, and empathizing with her. "So you're worried that he won't do as well on the state tests in March." "You're concerned that there are some topics I won't cover this year if I take time to do Morning Meeting every day." "You think that Morning Meeting is more for young children and that it's too baby-like for nine-year-olds."

[Date]

Dear Parents,

Next week your child will be taking the state-required proficiency tests. Your child will be tested in reading, writing, math, science, and citizenship. The tests aim to show what children know and can do in these areas compared with state standards and other students in their grade.

Some children and parents get nervous about these tests. It may help to think of the tests for what they are—just one measure of how a child is doing in school. To get a full picture of the child's learning, we need to look at his/her other schoolwork, abilities, knowledge, interests, and motivation. No one thing should stand alone as the indicator of a child's progress.

We have spent some time at school on test-taking strategies and ways to stay relaxed during the tests. This week we've been listing and charting all the things we know in these test subjects, so that the children will see how much knowledge they have and go into the tests feeling confident.

You can help your child have a successful testing week. Here are some tips:

1. Ask your child about the test-taking strategies we have been practicing in class and the techniques for relaxing if your child gets nervous during a test.

2. Remind your child to read and listen to all test-taking directions carefully and to ask questions if any directions are unclear.

3. Make sure your child gets plenty of sleep before the tests and is well-rested.

4. Make sure your child eats a good breakfast on the day of the test. Being hungry can make it hard for children to do well on tests.

6. Encourage your child to do his/her best.

Please call if you have any questions or concerns.

Sincerely,

[Teacher's name]

After listening to her, I presented her with some research about the connection between social skills and academic achievement. I reassured her, too, that academics are also emphasized in our Morning Meetings, and we decided together that she would come into the classroom on several occasions to see how that was accomplished. We agreed to talk again after these observations to see how she felt at that point.

After Nathan's mom observed a few of our Morning Meetings, she told me that she now understood the power in this approach and how much academics we cover during that time.

Not all differences of opinion between teacher and parents will be so smoothly resolved. In a small number of cases, other school staff will need to be pulled into conversation with the parent, or special exceptions will need to be made for a student, or the disagreement could linger on, never fully and satisfactorily resolved. The point is, sharing information with parents decreases the likelihood of disagreement, and disagreement should never be the result of lack of information.

Chapter Six

Spotlight:

Family Literacy Nights

Kindergarten through Second Grade
Penn Valley Elementary School
Levittown, Pennsylvania

"One of the biggest questions I get from parents is 'How can I help my child learn?'" says first and second grade teacher Judy Wentzel. It's a huge question, but she devised and hosted a program with her colleague Maryann Fedorko at Penn Valley Elementary School in Levittown, Pennsylvania, that got at part of the answer. They hosted literacy nights to show parents how their children were being taught reading and writing at school and to give parents fun ideas for how to help their children with these subjects at home.

The program, which won the school an award from the Pennsylvania Coalition for Parent Involvement, consisted of four Tuesday evenings of relaxed, low-pressure adult-child literacy games and activities. In the fall, all of the school's second graders and their families were invited to come to school for four Tuesdays. In the winter, a similar series was offered for all first grader families, and in the spring, a final series was offered for all kindergartner families. About ten families took up the offer in each case.

A typical night

Penn Valley's literacy nights had three components: literacy-based board games, writing, and story time.

Families would usually trickle in around 6:30. To make sure everyone had some constructive activity to do while waiting for other families to arrive, Judy and Maryann would set out brown envelopes filled with simple games that challenged players to recognize patterns or fill in missing letters in words. Adult-child pairs would settle quickly into these productive pastimes as more families arrived.

Once all the families were present, the whole group would move into the evening's featured board games. Two games were featured each week, and enough game sets were available for everyone to play simultaneously. One evening, one game was a literacy version of tic-tac-toe; the other was a take-off of Chutes and Ladders in which players, in order to advance a square, had to respond correctly to game cards that said things such as "Say a word that rhymes with *boy*" or "Say and clap the syllables in *burrito*." On other nights the games included take-offs of Bingo, Monopoly®, and other common games, all with a literacy slant.

After the games would come the writing portion of the evening. The teachers would show the children a collection of pictures as writing prompts. The children could choose whichever picture appealed to them and, with help from their parents, write something related to the picture. If the picture showed a beach, they could write down their memories of a past trip to the ocean, or describe how the picture made them feel. Younger children could dictate words for their parents to write.

Meanwhile, Judy and Maryann would circulate the room, here offering a word of encouragement, there modeling a way for an adult to help a child who's having trouble with the writing.

At the end of the writing time, any child who wanted to could come to the microphone to read his/her writing to the assembled audience of peers and adults, an activity designed to boost children's confidence.

Winding down the evening would be story time, designed to allow both the children and parents to experience the pleasure of listening to a story, and to allow the teachers to model how to read to a child. With children and adults all gathered around, one of the teachers would read, demonstrating the intonations, dramatic pauses, and facial expressions that bring a story to life. "You should've seen the parents," says Judy. "They were always as enthralled as the children."

At the end of each evening, there would be a book give-away. Several children's names would be drawn to receive a book to take home and keep, a strategy to encourage reading at home. The books came from a variety of sources—extras from the school library, freebies from the PTO book sale. By keeping track of whose name had been drawn, the teachers ensured that every child got at least one free book by the end of the four-week series.

Making it easy to do at home

A top goal in planning the literacy nights was to make sure families could easily do similar activities at home, say Judy and Maryann. "We wanted to show parents how to use everyday things to help their children learn, so we didn't want to buy a lot of expensive stuff for the games," says Maryann. She and Judy therefore made all the game sets themselves, using simple index cards, oak tag, and other materials they had at hand or that they bought from a local dollar store. Judy adds, "We told parents, 'If your child has outgrown a board game, make

Chapter Six

up some simple game cards to use with that same board, and you've got a new game.'"

To further encourage families to play literacy games at home, the two teachers made enough game sets so that families could take two games home each week and then bring them back the following week in exchange for two more games. In addition, over the course of the four weeks, every family took home and kept at least two game boards and eight sets of game cards that could be used on those boards.

"It was time consuming to make all those games," says Maryann. "But it was so rewarding. To see parents sitting with their child, learning with their child, talking about consonant blends and vowels and rhymes and saying 'This is fun!'—It was enough to make you cry. I'd do it again in a heartbeat."

Spotlight:
Family
Literacy
Nights

A safe, relaxed atmosphere

If they had to name one crucial element to success with these literacy nights, say the teachers and parents alike, it was the safe, relaxed atmosphere of the gatherings. "Most of our time was spent playing," says Janet Fiatoa, who, with her husband, Mark, took turns coming to the literacy nights with their daughter. "The teachers made the whole evening feel so game-like. It never felt like a school setting."

The relaxed atmosphere not only made things fun, but it helped the children grow more confident about their reading and writing, says Janet. "In the first few weeks, not many children were willing to go to the mike to read their writing. By the end of the program even the shy children wanted to," she recalls.

Besides the focus on games, lots of small things contributed to this supportive atmosphere: the fact that it was the same group of families week after week; the fact that when children read their work to the audience, Judy would sit next to the more timid readers so they'd feel like they were just reading to her; the fact that if a reader stumbled on a word, she wouldn't make them sound it out or struggle in front of everyone, but simply supplied the word so the child could move on; and the fact that parents were welcome to bring their other children if they didn't have a babysitter that night.

For the Fiatoas, this all translated to important quality time with their daughter. Janet and Mark initially signed up for the literacy nights hoping to get advice on how to help their daughter with reading problems. What they got was that and more. "Looking back, the most important thing was that our daughter got quality one-on-one attention from the two of us," says Janet. "If it weren't for the literacy nights we still would've read to her every night, but this was so much more fun."

Adaptable for individual classrooms

Although at Penn Valley these literacy nights were for any student across a grade in the school, individual classroom teachers could easily organize something similar just for their classes, say Judy and Maryann. Teachers can design games and activities to fit whatever they're teaching in class.

The important thing, Judy and Maryann advise, is to have activities that families can easily replicate at home, and to consciously foster a safe, relaxed atmosphere.

Chapter Six

Chapter Seven

SHARING CHILDREN'S WORK WITH PARENTS

*ow important is it to see our son's schoolwork? On a scale of one to ten it's a twelve. It keeps us present with who he is in school. It gives us and the teacher a common language to speak because his work is something tangible that everyone can look at and comment on, whether it's to say something positive or to voice a concern.*

Parent of a kindergartner

It's a rare parent who can come to the classroom regularly all year long to see her/his child in action. To get an accurate picture of how their children are doing, then, parents need to see the children's work.

Ideally, teachers would show the work in a systematic and purposeful way. The work shared would support what the teacher would like to communicate about the child. The child would be involved in selecting the samples. And parents would have an easy way to communicate back to the teacher. Most importantly, work sharing would not be limited to the twice-yearly parent-teacher conferences, but would happen frequently and regularly throughout the year.

When I first started teaching, I was far from this ideal. I can remember having a pit in my stomach the morning of parent-teacher conferences. I was twenty-two years old and fresh out of college. Many of my students' parents were much older than I was. I would be showing them their child's grades during the conference, and I worried that some of them might challenge the grades that this young and inexperienced teacher was giving their child. If I had evidence to back up the grades, I'd be in a much better position. The problem was it was

November, and I should have been thinking about this back in August. Sure, I had collected a few work samples to bring out at conference time, but I'd picked these rather randomly. And yes, I had sent students' work home sporadically throughout the fall, but half the time I couldn't articulate what the work was meant to show.

I realized I had not been giving parents a very clear picture of what and how their child was doing in school. Furthermore, I had missed the opportunity to build relationships with parents in a fairly simple but meaningful way. And I had missed a chance to have the students become more actively involved in their own learning.

Gradually, I became more organized and purposeful. In this chapter I'll outline the broad guidelines I now have for myself in sharing students' work with parents. I'll then offer some specific ideas for accomplishing these broad goals.

**Guidelines
for Sharing
Students'
Work**

Guidelines for Sharing Students' Work

Think about your purpose

Clarify what you want to communicate overall to parents through showing children's work and what each piece of work is meant to illustrate.

Share children's work routinely throughout the year, not just at conference time

This helps lay the groundwork for open communication between teachers and parents. It allows teachers and parents to address any problems the child is having before they become too big. And it ensures that there are no surprises for anyone at conference time.

Communicate children's progress in academic and social learning

To get an accurate and vivid picture of the child's progress in school, parents need to know how their child is doing in developing both academic and social skills.

Share children's on-paper and non-paper work

From clay models to dioramas, there is much that children produce during a school day that is not on paper. Find ways to show such work to parents, such as taking photos of the work and sending them home or inviting parents to come see a display.

Give students an active role

Many teachers ask students to choose (with guidance) what to show their parents, to reflect in writing on the work they chose, and to do some of the actual sharing of the work with their parents. Giving students a significant role this way can make them better learners: It encourages them to monitor their own learning, appreciate all that they have learned, identify areas they need to improve upon, and figure out how to make those improvements.

Invite communication from parents about the child's work

To get the most out of sharing students' work, many teachers actively and explicitly invite parents to give comments—to the teacher and their child—about the work they were shown.

Ways to Share Children's Work

There are many practical ways to share children's work with their parents throughout the year and many ways to decide what should be shared. No one way is best for all teachers. Sometimes a combination of methods proves effective. Each teacher can decide what's appropriate by keeping his/her goals in mind and thinking about the strengths, interests, constraints, and preferences of the particular class of students and their parents.

Here are a few methods that teachers have used successfully:

Weekly work reviews

Many teachers send home some work sample or review once a week. Here are two manageable ways to do this:

Thursday Papers

In Chapter 4, I talked about Thursday Papers, a system in which students take home each week's schoolwork to show their parents. I described how this was a way for me to keep parents informed of what's going on in the classroom. But Thursday Papers are also a great way to give children an active role in sharing their work with parents and to encourage meaningful communication between the parent and child about schoolwork.

I begin by having the students reflect on their work each week and write down one thing they want their parents and me to notice or know about their work. Students can write about the contents of their work folders or about something that isn't shown in the on-paper samples. They can write about academic or social skills. For example, "I want you to notice how I remembered to carefully check back over my math problems," one student wrote. Others have written, "I want you to know that I have been working hard on staying in my seat during independent work periods," "I want you to notice how much I know about ecosystems," and "I want you to know that I've been working on being assertive by asking questions when I don't understand something." These statements are added to the folders that the children take home.

Once home, the children's task is to sit down and go over their folders with their parents, showing them their statement along with my comment and pointing out any work that illustrates those remarks. The parents then tell their children what they noticed about the work. Finally, the parents have the option of writing a comment about the child's work and adding it to the folder.

Ways to Share Children's Work

Of course, for all this to work, I need to teach and guide students proactively on how to reflect on their work and decide what's important for their parents to notice. I help children understand that while we should celebrate finished products of high quality, we should also make note of good effort. We should honestly reflect on mistakes and think about how we might do better next time. I give children opportunities to practice thinking about these things in different situations: when we choose work to display on our walls, when we offer comments on each other's draft writing, when we assess how our Morning Meeting went.

With the parents, too, it helps to take proactive steps to ensure that the time spent looking over their children's folder at home is productive and positive for everyone. At back-to-school night, I model and offer tips on how to talk with children about their work. I also send home a letter on the topic. A sample is on the facing page.

Reflection sheets

Many teachers have students fill out a reflection sheet at the end of each week and show it to their parents. You can have students do this along with taking home work samples from the week. See examples of reflection sheets beginning on page 144.

[Date]

Dear Parents,

Each week this year your child will be bringing home a folder of the week's work for you to look over. I hope you'll have a chance to sit down together and reflect on the contents of the folder.

Here are some tips for reviewing and talking with your child about his/her work:

- Read your child's statement on what s/he wants you to notice or know about the week's work. Look for evidence of this as you flip through the folder. Share what you find with your child.

- Point out other successes in the work samples.

- Be specific in your comments. For example: "Your drawing for your book report shows a lot of detail."

- After noting the positives, you might want to suggest one or two things for your child to work on.

I encourage you to write a one- or two-sentence positive comment about your child's work each week to be added to the folder.

Enjoy these work-sharing times with your child. If you have any questions, please feel free to contact me.

Sincerely,

[Teacher's name]

**Chapter
Seven**

Two second graders' reflection sheets

Ways to
Share
Children's
Work

Name A l e x S.   Date 10/15/04

My Week

This week I learned how to make a name insect.

One hard thing this week was finishing My Cricket journal.

One easy thing this week was morning work.

I had fun when we have P.E.

My goal next week is to finish my hardy boys (numb.2) book.

Name __Mariah__   Date __15__

My Week

This week I learned
about crickets.
_____
_____

One hard thing this week was
Waking up early to go
to School.
_____

One easy thing this week was
Packing up to go home.
_____
_____

I had fun when
* I went to recess.
_____
_____

My goal next week is to

to read better than
this week.

Two fourth graders' reflection sheets

The Week in Review

Name _Jennie_   Date _10-15-04_

Some interesting things I learned this week were

Some interesting things I learned this
week were the 5 regions of Virginia
and how to remember the cities that are close to the
rivers. (Alex like potatoes, Fred likes to rap and King James
is rich).

The part of the week that I enjoyed the most was

The part of the week I liked the
best was when everybody sang Happy
because Birthday to me.
I really liked that because
it was my birthday and it made
me feel good.

A problem I had was

A problem I had was I was talking
a lot.

I handled this by

I will handle this by concentrating
on my work and not talking.

I am most proud of the way I

I am most proud of the way I
finished my work on time.

A goal I have for next week is

My goal for next week is to not
use paper for silly things.

time they have a similar assignment. The following week, the students take the work down, put it in their pizza box along with the form, choose a piece of work from the current week, and the process starts again.

If students choose some work that can't be inserted into a pizza box, I take a photo of it and we put the photo in the box. I'm routinely taking pictures of sculptures of book characters, dioramas of ecosystems, pattern blocks showing the student's understanding of fractions, LEGO® structures of a story's setting, costumes and props from a play about pioneer life. The list goes on.

In addition to writing about their displayed work, the children have other opportunities to reflect on their learning. For example, after completing a project or as part of Academic Choice, they write about what they did, what they learned, what they are most proud of, what was hard or easy for them, what they might do differently next time, and what they liked or didn't like about the work. These self-evaluations, along with the work described (or a photo of it), are added to the pizza boxes as well.

To show progress in particular content areas

In addition to allowing students to choose items for their portfolios, I also dictate some types of work for inclusion to show progress in particular content areas. Here are some examples of required items:

Writing samples

Students choose samples of writing that they took from initial idea to final draft. Our class has a common rubric that the students and I use to evaluate writings. The student's evaluation and mine both go into the pizza box along with the writing samples that the student chooses.

Journals

Students keep a daily journal, writing on topics of their choice. The journal is also where they record reflections at the end of each day. I require students to include these journals regularly as a way to show changes in their writing over time.

Reading logs

Each time the children do any reading, in or out of school, they record their activity on a log sheet. This may sound laborious, but students like keeping the logs—and their parents like seeing them—as evidence of how much the children are reading.

Notes from book conferences

Each week I hold individual conferences with children on the book they're currently reading to assess their reading fluency and comprehension. As I listen to the child read and as the children answer my questions about the book, I take notes. Photocopies of these notes often go into the portfolios.

Parent–teacher conferences

Ways to Share Children's Work

Conferences remain a good opportunity to share children's work with parents. As I learned the hard way in my first years of teaching, these conferences go much better when parents have seen samples of their child's work all along and when there's a rhyme and reason to how these samples were chosen.

In addition, it's a good idea to create some type of format to follow, at least roughly, during the actual conference. The format should help you clearly articulate whatever it is you want to communicate without overwhelming the parents. I usually create a form like the one on the facing page to help me stay organized during the conference.

I fill out this form for each child before I meet with the parents. I also make a copy for the parents to use during the conference. This way they can take additional notes while we're talking and then have a record of our meeting.

Here's what each section of the form is for:

Current goals for child

These are goals for the current quarter that the parent, child, and I jointly decided on. They are often related to but more specific than the child's or parent's overall hopes and dreams for the entire year.

Areas of strength

These are areas that the child is doing well in, based on his/her reflections and mine. For each area of strength, I note work samples or other records that illustrate this strength. As the parents and I talk during the conference, we go through the child's pizza box, looking at the relevant samples. I also note relevant anecdotes that I want to be sure to share with the parents.

Parent-Teacher Conference

Child's name: Maria   Date: Nov. 15

Current goals for child:

1. Slowing down — more careful to read directions, check over work for accuracy, clarity, neatness

2. Staying focused during independent work periods

Areas of strength: Supporting work:

1. Reading - above grade level, different genres > Reading log, reading assessment, acad. choice projects on books read

2. Friendly to all children > Anecdotes: Bobby at recess, Lisa during Choice time

3. Math - figuring out diff. ways to solve problems > Math journal, anecdotes from Math Choice time

Improvements needed: Supporting work:

1. Continue to work on proofreading work > Journal, 2 writing samples, science test, math work

2. Adding more to work - has been doing just enough to get by > Science acad. choice project, writing samples

Goals for next term:

1. Proofreading <u>all</u> work. Slowing down.

2. Adding more details to produce quality work.

3. Continue to focus during independent work times.

Additional notes:

Parents' support with helping Maria check over homework. Using checklist to help Maria.
Any other ideas from parents?

Conference notes:

- Mom says Maria taking responsibility for setting timer and getting work done at home without being reminded.

- Get checklists to parents for Maria to put in homework box at home.

Chapter Seven

Improvements needed

Here I list areas for the child to continue working on, again along with illustrative work samples and classroom anecdotes.

Goals for next term

The student, parents, and I decide on these together. Sometime before the conference, the students look through their pizza box portfolio from the past quarter and name a goal to work toward during the next quarter. I record that goal, along with a goal that I have for the child. Then, at the conference, the parents add their goal for the child to the chart. Often there is considerable overlap between the three perspectives. I write these three goals (or a consolidation of them) on this sheet. These then become the "Current goals for child" on the following quarter's sheet.

**Ways to
Share
Children's
Work**

Additional notes

If there is anything else I want to discuss with the parents, I jot it down here. Sometimes it's a note to ask them for ideas for helping their child with a challenge at school. Often it's a reminder to thank them for something helpful they've been doing.

Conference notes

I leave this section blank before the conference. During the conference the parents and I write notes here about things we discussed or about any follow-up work we might need to do.

After the conference, I invite parents to take their child's pizza box portfolio home for a few days so they can spend time looking through its contents with their child.

(To learn about another idea for structuring conferences, see "Student-Led Conferences" on the facing page.)

Benefits Parents, Students, and Teachers

Sharing children's work with parents gives all involved—the parent, student, and teacher—something tangible to focus on when talking about the child's learning. For parents, the work samples help paint a picture of their child at school. For students, the work sharing is encouragement to become invested in their own learning. For teachers, the process offers a manageable way of communicating with parents about their children's progress clearly and systematically.

Spotlight:

Student-Led Conferences:
A New Twist on a Familiar School Routine

Fifth Grade, East Hill Elementary School, Camillus, New York
and
Third Grade, Poplar Tree Elementary School, Chantilly, Virginia

Chapter Seven

It's late October, and fifth grader Wen and his dad have just arrived at school for a conference with the teacher. Soft music is playing as they walk into the classroom. Over on a table there's light finger food that the teacher brought in. In a clear but slightly nervous voice, Wen introduces the adults to each other: "Dad, this is Mr. Shaw. Mr. Shaw, this is my dad." When the adults have shaken hands and exchanged pleasantries, Wen invites his dad to sign the classroom guest book before the three sit down for a conversation about Wen's learning. "Thank you for coming to this conference," Wen starts.

So begins a student-led conference in fifth grade teacher Patrick Shaw's classroom at East Hill Elementary School in Camillus, New York. Used in many elementary schools, student-led conferences differ from the traditional type in several ways: Before each conference, the student evaluates his/her growth since the last conference, the student decides what accomplishments and goals to highlight during the conference, and the student leads the conversation at the actual conference. In short, student-led conferences put children at the center of the process, encouraging them to become self-directed learners.

Benefits of the approach

Educators experienced with student-led conferences cite several benefits. First, it challenges children to take responsibility for their own learning, and most rise to the occasion. When teachers explain the purpose of the approach and offer guidance on self-assessment and goal-setting, students tend to evaluate their performance with honesty and to set appropriate goals for themselves.

Another benefit cited is that student-led conferences keep the adults focused on the child. With the child in the room and in the center of the conversation, the adults are more likely to focus on the specific needs of this child at this time, rather than talking about general educational concepts, their own experiences as students, or other issues not immediately relevant to the child.

For families whose home language is not English, there's the additional benefit that the child can conduct the meeting in the family's home language. Patti Kinney, who has written a book on student-led conferences, says, "The language is no longer a problem, so [non-English speaking parents] feel much more comfortable attending." Teachers need not worry if they don't know the language that the family will be using, she says. "The student can act as a translator if needed, and it's amazing how much [teachers] can pick up from expression and body language... It's pretty easy to tell if the student is giving the parent the accurate picture." (Gordon 2003)

Parents typically approve of student-led conferences, say teachers who have tried it. Jeanne Gabris, parent of one of Patrick's students, says, "The student-led conferences gave me a lot of feedback. My kids knew what their strengths and weaknesses were, and they were super honest about them. And I always felt I knew the details of what was going on with them academically and socially."

Spotlight: Student-Led Conferences

But what if a parent wants to talk with the teacher, or vice versa, without the child present? Using student-led conferences does not mean those private conversations can't happen. Many teachers welcome parents to schedule a private follow-up conversation if they wish. Teachers, likewise, can ask parents for a private conversation, or they can use student-led conferences in combination with traditional parent-teacher conferences.

While student-led conferences can take more teacher time than traditional conferences—most teachers schedule twenty to thirty minutes per family, a little longer than traditional conferences—the extra time is well worth it, say many teachers. "I don't mind spending the extra time," says Patrick. "It's what's right for kids, and it's made my teaching easier."

Elements of student-led conferences

While the details of student-led conferences vary from classroom to classroom and grade to grade, they usually include the following elements:

Introducing the concept to students and parents

Because student-led conferences are a new concept to many children and families, it's important for the teacher to introduce the idea carefully. Teacher Ramona McCullough, who has used the method successfully with her third graders, brings up the topic to children during the first weeks of school, then returns to it frequently throughout the year. She explains the process and emphasizes the children's role of honestly assessing their own work, deciding what improvements to try to make, and thinking about how their parents and teacher can help them make those improvements. Depending on the children's age, Ramona says, teachers using this approach may need to take time to help children grasp concepts such as "goals," "quality," "accomplishment," "effort," and "challenge."

Parents, too, benefit from a careful introduction to the idea early in the school year—at back-to-school night or the first open house, for example. In her presentations, Ramona emphasizes the value of students assessing their own work. "Our own assessment is often more thoughtful than others'," she tells parents. "We're also more accepting of our own assessment. When children are asked to evaluate their own work," she says, "they grow and learn because they want to, not because someone else told them to."

The student portfolio

A central element of student-led conferences is the student portfolio, a collection of the student's work that shows what the student has learned and what s/he still needs to work on. During the conference, the student, parent, and teacher look through the portfolio together. The portfolio focuses the conversation and encourages everyone to talk about specific examples and details of the child's progress.

Although the contents of these portfolios vary by classroom and grade, typically the student is involved in choosing which items to include.

Here's what Ramona's third graders put into their portfolios:

One work sample per week

Each Friday morning, the children choose one piece of work from the week that they feel represents something important about their learning. Ramona offers guidance, encouraging children to choose from various subjects and to consider not only work that represents accomplishment, but work that represents effort and challenge.

A written reflection about the work chosen

After choosing their work sample, the children write about why they chose it and what they want others to notice about it. As part of her reflection about a work sample, one child wrote, "I used every brain power possible on this, even though I know it doesn't show. It was a real challenge."

A written reflection about the quarter overall

Ramona's class has conferences each quarter. Just before each conference, the children think about their learning over the past quarter as a whole and write an overall reflection. "I have improved a lot," one student wrote. "The 3rd quarter was a little easier academically. I tried very hard and have accomplished something. I like to write and read now." (See page 158 for a fifth grader's quarterly reflection sheet.)

A goals sheet

A week or two before the end of each quarter, each child names three goals, academic or social, to work on during the next quarter. The parents are asked to name three goals for their child, and the teacher also names three goals for the child. The child then chooses three goals out of the nine to work on. It's usually not hard to choose, Ramona says, because there typically is overlap between the goals everyone names. (See sample goals sheet on page 157.)

Spotlight:
Student-Led
Conferences

The conference itself

The conference itself is the culmination of the work evaluations and reflections that the student has been doing all quarter. Typically at the conference, the child reads any overall reflections s/he wrote and chooses a few of the work samples from the portfolio to highlight. "This is my proudest work from this quarter," the child might say. "I gave it 100 percent. It was my best work in social studies." The child then points out details of the assignment that s/he wants the parent to notice. Finally, s/he talks about the goals to work on for the next quarter.

Though these conferences are meant to be friendly and relaxed, the children need a certain amount of poise to keep the conversation focused and productive. Rehearsal, therefore, is vital. "I model for the students and then have them role play before the conference," says Patrick, the fifth grade teacher. The students get in groups of two or three. One or two students take the role of the parents, while the last student plays him/herself. The group rehearses the conference, complete with looking through the portfolio and highlighting specific pieces of work. Then the students switch roles. "I always find that because the students did such a good job practicing, I don't need to say much at the real conference," says Patrick. "I serve as a supporter and clarifier."

The family then takes the portfolio home to look at its contents in detail. Some time later, the portfolios are returned to school so that children can add the next quarter's contents.

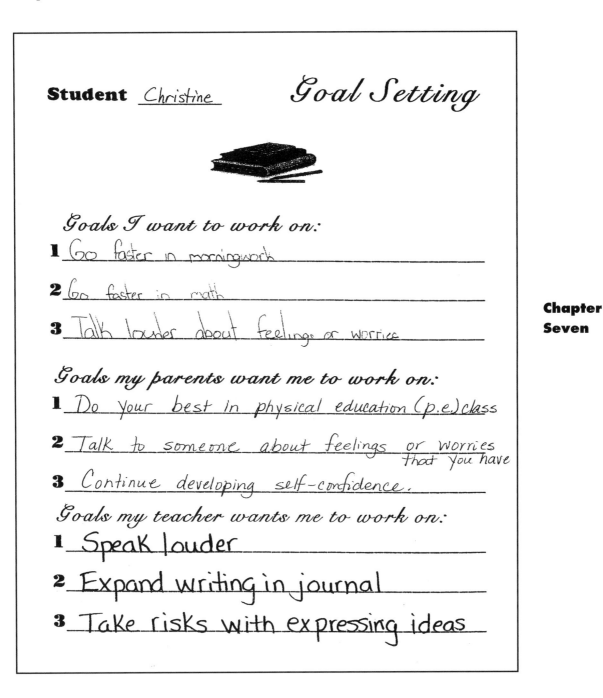

Student <u>Christine</u> *Goal Setting*

Goals I want to work on:

1 Go faster in morningwork

2 Go faster in math

3 Talk louder about feelings or worries

Goals my parents want me to work on:

1 Do your best in physical education (p.e.) class

2 Talk to someone about feelings or worries that you have

3 Continue developing self-confidence.

Goals my teacher wants me to work on:

1 Speak louder

2 Expand writing in journal

3 Take risks with expressing ideas

Chapter Seven

*In one classroom, the children, parents, and teacher each name three goals
for the student. Out of the nine, the student chooses three to work on.
In other classrooms, only the student names goals for him/herself.*

Spotlight: Student-Led Conferences

Dear Mom and Dad,

This past quarter I did well in this/these subject(s): Social Studies and Spelling.

What helped me do well was I worked hard and we played Jeperdy.

I found Math to be difficult subject(s) this quarter because it was so much harder than I was used to doing Math.

I have shown improvement in Writing.

My proudest moment this quarter was When I got a 100 in social studies because I like to get 100s. It makes me feel like I know a lot.

One thing you may not know about me at school is I like school a little.

When you look at my portfolio, please notice Social Studies. I worked hard in that subject.

Here are the goals I reached last quarter:
I improved in math.
Take more time in writing
talk less

In some classrooms, the student's overall reflection about the quarter is in the form of a fill-in-the-blank letter to the parents. This one is from a fifth grader.

My goals for the next quarter are:

1. Work on math
2. Keep good behavior
3. Work more on State project

You can help me reach my goals by Make sure I
Study more when I have to.

Signed,

Alex

Post-conference reflections

After the conference, the children write a brief reflection of how the meeting went. "My conference went well because I went slowly and got everything done...I think my parents really listened carefully and paid attention to what I said," one fifth grader wrote.

In many classes, the parents also write a reflection in the form of a letter to their child. Parents may appreciate suggestions on what kind of things to write. For example, teachers might offer a list of sentence prompts, such as "I noticed that...," "I'm proud of...," "Keep up the good work on...," "I know that sometimes you have difficulty with...but...," "I'm glad to see you're working hard on..." and "I can help by...."

"The parent letters are the most powerful piece of the process," says Patrick. "The letters are so touching. I often suggest that kids pull out their portfolios and reread their parents' letters during quiet time. Often when they're a little sad, reading the letters seems to make them feel better."

One parent's post-conference letter to his child is on page 160.

Although student-led conferences require teachers and parents to make a shift from what they're used to, many teachers and families find them less stressful than traditional parent-teacher conferences. "You're taking a time that could be really threatening, and you're lowering the level of stress," Patrick says. Third grade teacher Ramona McCullough summarizes, "The students feel ownership of their learning, parents feel that they are a part of the process, and I get to see what the students are thinking about their learning."

Spotlight: Student-Led Conferences

Dear Ryan,

I was proud of the way you presented to me what you do in school and those things that interested you. Even though you were nervous I could tell that you had given a lot of thought about what you needed to say.

You are very smart in math. You enjoy it and it comes so easy to you. You may not know it, but one day you will benefit a great deal from math. Even though social studies isn't your favorite subject, you still should work hard at it. Always do your best at whatever you do.

I know I am very busy and sometimes I don't seem to have enough time to help you with everything you need help with. If it's really important to you or your school work, don't be afraid to tell me so. I will do whatever I need to help you.

Keep up the good work, Ryan! I am very proud of you and your accomplishments! You are a good student and a great person with a lot to offer other people. I love you!

Dad

Chapter Eight

PROBLEM SOLVING WITH PARENTS

I*f my child is having problems,*
I would want the teacher to help me find the right resources to help her.
If teachers and parents work together, we can address any problem a child has.

Parent of a sixth grader

Despite our best proactive efforts, it's inevitable that problems will arise for some children in the course of the year—behavior issues, academic struggles, or a combination of the two. When that happens, the child's parents can be invaluable partners in addressing the problems.

This chapter will offer ideas for problem solving with parents. First, though, I want to emphasize the importance of establishing a positive relationship with parents before any problem comes up. We're all more willing to work on difficult problems with people we know and trust, and parents are no different. Effective problem solving requires brainstorming, give-and-take, and open-minded solution seeking. For parents to be willing to invest in this kind of hard work, they need to know that the teacher respects them, respects their child, and appreciates their child as a unique individual.

Having a foundation of trust and understanding can also simply reduce stress—for the parent and the teacher. When a child is having a problem, parents may feel angry, afraid, or frustrated. There could be a variety of reasons: Perhaps they think they'll be blamed as bad parents. Maybe they speak a different language or a different English dialect than the teacher or are confused by the school bureaucracy. Possibly they've had a history of stressful contacts with schools or they carry unhappy memories of school from their own childhood. Teachers, meanwhile, may have their own stresses. They may fear being blamed as incompetent teachers, feel daunted by the tasks ahead, or simply be exhausted. For teachers and parents alike, knowing they have a partner in each other rather than an adversary can cushion some of these feelings.

Just as importantly, a relationship of trust and cooperation between the parent and teacher can reduce stress for the child. Children who are struggling in school often feel afraid, disoriented, discouraged, or embarrassed. Seeing their parent and their teacher working together on their side, cooperating to solve the problem, can be reassuring.

Using the proactive strategies discussed in the previous chapters of this book can help teachers build the prerequisite positive relationship with parents. As behavior support specialist Kathryn Brady says, "The prep for the 'hard times' begins when the teacher asks parents about their hopes and dreams for their child back in August or September, and it continues with every positive interaction after that." With that foundation laid, parents and teachers can work together better when a problem emerges.

On the Same Side as Parents

On the Same Side as Parents

Problem solving with parents requires getting on the same side with them to focus on helping the child. So often, when feeling frustrated or stressed, teachers and parents both get into a blaming, adversarial stance. We've all heard it before—from ourselves and others: *This is what I'm trying to teach the child. If the parents would just cooperate, everything would be fine.* Or: *My child is fine at home. She has problems at school because the teacher isn't working with her right.* But if we're to have any hope of solving problems effectively with parents, we have to transcend this mentality and set a tone of "Let's figure out together how we can help the child."

I find that it helps to remind myself, especially when tensions rise and my patience is low, that parents are an important ally because they know and love their child and are even more invested in his/her success than I am. They have a history with the child that I haven't had and a life with the child that I don't share. They may see gifts in the child that I never have the opportunity to witness. Hearing about all this can help me see the problem in a different light. Parents also know of things going on at home that could help explain the problems at school. Maybe a stay-at-home parent has gone back to work, maybe a parent has lost a job, maybe a sibling is sick, maybe the child is running around with an older group of kids in the neighborhood. I remind myself that I need information and wisdom from parents in order to help their child.

Of course problem solving is a two-way street. We need parents to see us, too, as allies rather than adversaries. This chapter offers some steps and some language for teachers to use to encourage a collaborative mindset in parents. But those steps will feel false to parents, and the suggested language will ring hollow, if they're not undergirded by our true desire to work on the same side with parents. Conversely, if we truly do want to work on the same side with them, they'll know it, even if our steps or our words aren't always exactly right.

A Repertoire of Problem Solving Strategies

When a student is having a problem in school, teachers need to have a repertoire of ways to work on it with the child's parents. Below are some suggestions, ranging from sending a brief note to the parents, to holding a group meeting of the parents, teacher, administrators, and other adults.

Although teachers generally start with the simplest steps and progress to more complicated ones as needed, there's no rule about this. Good problem solving is as much art as science. The same response will not work for all students or for the same student at different times. Successful teachers use their intuition as much as any set protocol in deciding which strategies to use.

Call or write a brief note when you first notice a possible problem

Describe what you've noticed in a concrete and factual way, but keep the tone relaxed and reassuring. For example: "Looks like Aden might have had a tough day. He made some rude comments to classmates at recess today. We resolved it and everything's okay, but I just wanted to let you know so we can both keep an eye on this." It may turn out that Aden was just having an off day, or it could be the start of a bigger problem. In either case, most parents appreciate being kept in the loop.

Call again or send another note if the problem persists

Elaborate on the problem and ask the parent for help in addressing it. Again, stick to the facts rather than making a judgment. For example: "Aden is still facing some challenges in being friendly with other children. He grabbed some game pieces out of a classmate's hands today and later pushed a classmate in line" instead of "Aden is still being troublesome." In asking parents for help, be clear that you're doing just that, not telling the parents what to do. For example: "I'm wondering if you have ideas for how to work with Aden to be gentler with other children."

Meet with the parents to talk about the problem

As with notes and phone calls, it's important that in meetings with parents, teachers convey a desire to work *with* them to help the child. Seeking and listening to parents' perspective is key. The section "Tips for Successful Problem Solving" on the next page offers some suggestions.

**Have a problem solving conference
with the child and tell the parents about it**

In a problem solving conference, the teacher involves the child in finding solutions to the problem. The teacher helps the child note his/her strengths and challenges, identify and understand the problem, state his/her point of view, generate possible solutions, and choose one solution to try. Filling the parents in on the conference allows them to support the child in trying the chosen solution. It also shows the child that the teacher and the parents are united in their desire to help the child resolve the issue. (For more on problem solving conferences, see Appendix D.)

A Repertoire of Problem Solving Strategies

**Work with the parents to set up an
individual contract for the child**

An individual contract is one way for the teacher and parents to join together to give a child the extra support s/he might need to change persistent problem behaviors. An individual contract states one or two behavior goals for the child. Unlike the child's or parents' broad hopes and dreams for the year or their goals for each quarter, these goals are specific to addressing the particular behavior problem the child is having now. The contract also defines a clear and concrete system for marking progress toward these specific goals, and states agreed-upon ways for the parents to celebrate with the child when the goals have been met. (For an example, see "An Individual Contract" on page 174.)

**Seek outside help if you need it,
and encourage parents to do the same**

The teacher, the parents, or both may sometimes want to bring others into a problem solving meeting. Especially when there's no obvious answer to the problem, outside help can be valuable. The teacher may want to bring in the school's behavior support specialist, a counselor, the principal, or the child's teacher from the previous year. The family may have a counselor, mentor, or tutor that they would like to have present. All these people can provide expertise, insight, and support.

Tips for Successful Problem Solving

Whether you're calling parents to talk about a child's problem, meeting with them, or filling them in on a problem solving conference you had with the child, here are some tips that can make the process go more successfully:

Address issues before they become a crisis

It's easier to solve a small problem than a big one. Whenever possible, let parents know of any difficulty their child may be having before the problem reaches a crisis level. Most children show some early warning signals of struggle— a couple of missing homework assignments, some disrespectful comments to the teacher, or picking on a classmate on the playground. This is the time to communicate with the parent. When I first began teaching, I thought that by contacting parents at the first warning sign, I was making a big deal out of nothing. I didn't want to bother parents. I soon learned that they would rather be "bothered" by a small issue than surprised by a problem that had been allowed to mushroom. As first grade teacher Maureen Russell in Springfield, Massachusetts, says, "If I'm asking myself 'Should I call?' it means I should."

Set up a time to talk without distractions

If the issue needs more than a short phone call or note, set up an appointment to talk. Don't engage in an extended conversation on the spot, such as during dropoff, pickup, or at an open house, even if the parents bring up an issue. Express your concern and make a separate time to talk so that both of you will be prepared, relaxed, and able to focus on the issue without distractions.

Focus on one or two issues for the moment

If there are several problems to solve, find one or two that you and the parent agree are most important to work on for the moment. I'm often tempted to try to remedy the entire situation at once, but I have to remind myself that I risk taking on more than I can handle and not making satisfactory progress on anything. Moreover, when teachers come to parents with a long list of things for the child to work on, the parents may feel they're being seen as a failure. Understandably, they often shut down, and the problem solving process comes to a halt. It's better to address fewer issues so that the teacher, parents, and child can all experience success in resolving them.

Let parents know you appreciate the child

Before talking about the problem, say something to let the parents know that you see, know, and care about their child. This is so important to parents. Researcher J. Hauser-Cramm wrote after interviewing many parents:

> "Parents used teacher's knowledge of their child's personality or interests as a screening device... a means of determining whether or not they were going to grant the teacher credibility. If they decided that a teacher did, in fact, appreciate their child's uniqueness, then they were much more willing to value a teacher's comments about the child's academic skills and even impressions that may not be entirely positive." (Swap 1993, 88)

Our noting of a child's positive qualities does not need to be a lengthy narrative. Something brief but specific will do: "Jason often reaches out to a classmate who has difficulty making friends," we might say. Or "Sally shows a lot of empathy for others. She shares her snack with anyone who forgot theirs" or "Coco works so hard during math time." This lets the family know that despite the problems that the child is having right now, the teacher still notices and appreciates the child's positive traits.

Collect documentation of the problem

As soon as I notice the early signs of a problem in a child, I begin observing carefully and keeping documentation. This documentation—samples of the child's work, anecdotes, notes from my observations, tallies of behavioral incidents—will be critically helpful as I work with the parent and child to resolve the issue. As education professor Sara Lawrence-Lightfoot points out, concrete documentation can help teachers tell—and help parents hear—hard truths. She writes:

> ...parents recoil at negative appraisals of their children that are not grounded in "artifacts, anecdotes, or evidence." Such generalized statements make them worry that the teacher doesn't like their child or is unfairly picking on him or her, and parents are likely to feel diminished or defensive. Yet when teachers are able to embed their concerns and criticisms in an evocative illustration or concrete evidence from student work, then parents may experience discomfort or disappointment, but they are better able to hear and respond to the teacher's concerns. They and the teacher can begin to problem-solve together. (Lawrence-Lightfoot 2003, 106)

Pay attention to language

Our language makes a huge difference in how successful we are in addressing problems with parents. Here are some things to remember:

Be brief and direct when stating the problem

Perhaps it's because it's hard to give negative news, but we teachers tend to go on and on in an attempt to justify our position to the last detail. Or we soften the news and end up being so vague that parents don't know what our point is. As first grade teacher Maureen Russell says, "Early in my career I was so afraid of offending parents that I'd sugarcoat everything." It's far better to state the problem briefly and directly. For example, we might say, "Megan is having a hard time with self-control" or "Megan is not getting her work done."

Back up the statement with one or two examples

"Megan is having a hard time with self-control. In math yesterday, she called out fifteen times in twenty minutes," we might say. The specific example lets parents know that we really have been watching and paying attention, and it provides a concrete place from which to begin solving the problem.

It can take courage to be direct with parents. Preparing what to say ahead of time, rehearsing with a colleague, and listening to experienced teachers talking with parents can all help. So can remembering that "parents are just people like you and me," says Maureen. Ultimately, most parents would prefer to hear direct language so they can understand the problem clearly.

Use "we" to show joint concern and responsibility

"We" is the most powerful word teachers can use when problem solving with parents. For example: "How can we solve this problem?" "What do we want as a goal for your child?" "What are we already doing?" "What could we be doing differently?" Using "we" lets families know they are not being judged and that the teacher shares the responsibility and accountability for the problem.

Ask before offering suggestions

If we want to offer parents some suggestions for things to try at home, we can first ask whether they'd like the suggestions. For example: "Would you like to hear what other families in your same situation have tried?" If, instead of asking first, we launch right into our suggestions, we risk coming across as if we're telling parents what to do. Asking whether parents would like to know what other families have done also lets them know that they're not alone, that other families have had similar problems. When asked whether they'd like some suggestions, most parents will say yes. And if they say no, we should respect that choice and understand that perhaps they'd prefer to work things out themselves or go to other sources for guidance.

Ask questions to get the parents' point of view

The value of learning parents' point of view cannot be overstated. Parents can shed important light on a child's situation. One teacher tells of working with a student named Jake who was having behavior problems. The teacher knew that Jake had first come to the family as a foster child and then was adopted, and she knew that the child had some psychological problems. But she didn't know the extent until the mother sat down and filled her in. The teacher learned of the child's malnutrition and serious neglect with the biological family and about the lengths his adoptive mother had gone to in trying to deal with his psychological issues. The mother also explained the patterns she had noticed in what triggered Jake's flare-ups. All this was important information that affected how the teacher would work with the child and parent.

Asking open-ended questions is a good way to invite parents' input, insights, and expertise. "What have you tried at home that seems to work for you?" we might ask. "What should I know about James that would help me?" "How can I better connect with Jiana?" "Can you think of some things I could do differently at school to help Makayla?" This lets the parents know that we value their wisdom.

Like all teachers, I sometimes feel convinced that a child is having problems because of something that's being done or not being done at home. However, I have to remind myself that more often than not, I don't have the complete story. I try to ask parents questions to avoid jumping to conclusions: "When does Sam go to bed?" "When does Halie do her homework?" "What are Joey's weekends like?" Often the answers enlighten me, telling me I did in fact rush to the wrong conclusion. Asking also allows parents to draw their own conclusions and come up with possible solutions: "She does her homework after dinner. She does seem tired then. Maybe I should have her do her homework before dinner and see if her work improves." The conclusion is more powerful coming from parents than from me.

Tips for Successful Problem Solving

Show empathy

It can be very frustrating and overwhelming for parents when their child is having a problem in school. As teachers, we can communicate to parents that we empathize with their situation. "I can imagine how frustrating this must be," we might say, or "It can be overwhelming to hear all this." As parents share their point of view, we can show empathy by paraphrasing with short statements such as "So you're saying you're really concerned about…," or by offering reassurance such as "I see how hard you've been working on this…" Nodding, avoiding crossing our arms, and using other nonthreatening body language can make a big difference, too. Parenting can be one of the most challenging jobs anyone will ever have. Acknowledging this and crediting parents for the hard work they're doing seem to lift a tremendous weight off their shoulders and help them be more emotionally ready to work on a problem.

Many times parents are angry and spill out all that's bothering them. I find it's important not to take what they're saying personally, but to let them vent while I take in any useful information. I try to say things like "I understand" and "I see" rather than get pulled into a debate. Empathic paraphrasing is also helpful in diffusing these situations. "I hear how this makes you angry…" When parents feel heard instead of attacked, they are usually more able to funnel their energy into problem solving.

Thank parents for working on the problem

"Having empathy for parents involves understanding that they may have taken time off work to meet with us and may have paid a fare to get to a meeting," says Kathryn Brady, who specializes in teaching children with social and emotional difficulties. "For all that parents do to solve problems with us, whether it involves bending to our schedule, spending money, talking to their child about an issue, or being willing to try a new routine, we should thank them clearly and genuinely."

Try to include the child in some part of the conversation

Children are more likely to be invested in solving the problem when they know what the teacher and parents are saying about it and have a voice in the problem solving. Having the child present in the process can also keep everyone focused on helping the child, instead of veering off into assigning, or defending against, blame.

A good time to include younger children might be after the adults have decided on a basic course of action. The child may be invited to decide on one or two details of carrying out the plan. With older students, it might be appropriate to bring them in during the problem solving conversations. Decide what works best for you, the particular parents, the particular child, and the situation at hand.

(For an example of involving the student in a problem solving process, see "An Individual Contract" on page 174.)

Know when to have support

So often in the teaching profession, we feel we need to bravely go it alone. The truth is we don't need to and we shouldn't try. Sometimes the wisest and most responsible thing is to bring others into the problem solving process, such as by consulting another professional or by calling a group together to talk about the problem. In these situations, it's important to realize that needing to rely on others is not a failure on the part of the teacher, but a reality of teaching.

Similarly, when parents want to bring others to a meeting, it's important to remember that needing to rely on others is also a fact of parenting. The more comfortable and supported both the teacher and parent feel in the problem solving process, the better off everyone is, beginning with the child.

Your schools may have guidelines or a policy on when teachers should bring others to a meeting with parents. In addition, you can ask yourself some questions: "Is there someone else who knows the child or the parent?" "Is there someone who's experienced at working with this type of problem?" "Will the parent feel more comfortable with someone else at the table?" "Will I be able to communicate better with a supportive colleague present?" "Do I feel emotionally or physically unsafe being alone with this parent?" Certainly if the answer to the last question is yes or even maybe, you should have others present.

If you bring others to the meeting, be sensitive to the possibility of the parent feeling bombarded or ganged up on. Let the parent know ahead of time that you'll be asking others to the meeting and stress that your goal is to have more good ideas for solving the problem. Explain what each person's role is.

In addition, all participants in the meeting should arrive and leave at the same time as the parent. Imagine how unnerving it must be for a parent to walk into the room only to see a group of "experts" already gathered and talking—presumably about the family. How unsettling as well to get up to leave at the end of the meeting while the rest of group lingers, looking like now they'll *really* talk, now that the parent is out of earshot. If the group must have any pre- or

Tips for Successful Problem Solving

post-meeting conversations without the parent present, have them on another day. If this isn't possible, the teacher should at least step out for a few minutes with the parent upon the parent's arrival or departure, see how s/he is feeling, and offer explanations and reassurances.

The Faith to Keep Trying

Sometimes good solutions come out of conversations with parents: There was Allie, who threw tantrums whenever she had to do hard schoolwork. Her parents and the teacher together devised a plan to allow Allie to do special fun artwork if she got through a week without tantrums. The tantrums diminished dramatically. There was Nick, whose teacher suggested that he stay in her inclusion classroom all day rather than be taken out for special instruction several times a day. The parents agreed, and the child's behavior improved. Finally there was Fong. At her parent's request, her teacher began sending a brief daily email about Fong's day so the parent could provide more immediate and constant support. Again the child's schoolwork and behavior improved.

Chapter Eight

Sometimes, however, the problem isn't easily resolved despite our best efforts, or it gets better for awhile, then gets worse again. This happens even to the most experienced teachers. It happens because teachers, parents, and children are human beings, and human beings are complex, and because problem solving is a complex undertaking with factors beyond our control. Jake's story is an example. The informative meeting the teacher had with Jake's mother took place in early fall. For two months the teacher sent notes to the mother, was on positive terms with her, and Jake's behavior remained stable. "I thought we were out of the woods," recalls the teacher. Then one day Jake had a setback at school. The teacher called to let the mother know and to ask whether something had happened that day at home to trigger the setback, only to have the mother react defensively, unable or unwilling to offer any helpful information. "To this day, I don't know what happened, if anything, that day to affect Jake," the teacher says. Tense conversations and unexpected shifts in feelings between parents and teachers can happen "even if we think we did everything right," she comments. It could be something the teacher did, but it could just as easily be something that had nothing to do with the teacher which the parent doesn't want to share.

When things don't go well, the best thing we can do is keep trying. Without blaming ourselves or the parents, we can move forward with faith that problems can be solved, if not with one swift effort, then in small steps that add up to change over time.

Spotlight:

An Individual Contract

Kindergarten
Southern Aroostook Community School
Dyer Brook, Maine

Spotlight: An Individual Contract

Tiffany, a kindergartner, was aggressive with the other children. She pushed and shoved to make room for herself in meeting circles, grabbed things out of other children's hands, and refused to share the snack bowl. She also had trouble following her teacher's directions. When told to come to the circle, she would take ten minutes to arrive, dawdling at every table, book shelf, and chair along the way.

Her teacher, Arlene Flye, had tried all the usual methods to work with Tiffany. She had carefully taught and modeled expected behaviors to the whole class since the first week of school. She gave Tiffany reminders and redirection whenever needed. She talked often with the child's parents about her behavior and, together with them, had set specific behavior goals for the child. When none of that made a lot of difference, Arlene decided to try an individual contract.

Based on a strategy described by teacher Ruth Sidney Charney in *Teaching Children to Care,* a "contract" is a nonpunitive strategy in which the teacher and parents work together to provide the extra structure and support that some children need in order to develop new behaviors. In a contract, the teacher and parents set up one or two behavior goals that address the problem at hand, along with a concrete system to encourage, mark, and celebrate success in meeting the goals. Contracts "focus on a child's strengths and capacity for self-control rather than giving negative orders—orders telling the child what not to do," writes Charney. "Offering a firm but matter-of-fact structure for expectations, a contract can dissipate the negativity that builds up after repeated reminders, nagging, and punishment." (Charney 2002, 340, 360)

Contracts are not a quick fix or the automatic default solution when a child has a problem. Often a simple phone call or a face-to-face meeting with the parents to talk about the problem is enough. In some cases, more involved measures are needed, possibly including diagnostic referrals for the child, resources for the family, or other services outside the purview of the classroom teacher. A contract is just one strategy for classroom teachers to try when a child's problem is difficult or persistent.

Elements of a contract

Behavioral goal statement

Contracts begin with a statement that clearly names concrete behavioral goals for the child, along with the reason for these goals. Unlike the broad hopes and dreams for the year or the quarterly goals, these goals are specific to solving the problem the child is having at the moment. The goals should be realistic: For example, if it's obvious that the child will not be able to complete homework every day, the goal might be to complete two homework assignments each week. The goals should also be clearly measurable: The teacher, student, and parents should be able to agree without argument about whether the goals were reached.

In Tiffany's case, Arlene felt the child could handle two simple goals, and the parents agreed. Tiffany's contract said she would "do her teachers' words" and "use friendly words and actions to share space and materials." (See "Tiffany's Contract" on the next page.)

Goal statements—and the fact that the child is using the individual contract strategy—are private matters that are not shared with the rest of the class. Sometimes students, especially in the younger grades, decide themselves to tell their classmates. "But I never encourage it, nor do I make a big deal of it if the child does tell others," says Arlene. The important thing is that teachers not share the information with the class.

A tangible marker of progress

Contracts rely on the teacher, student, and parents communicating consistently about the child's progress in meeting the behavioral goals. Usually this involves the teacher noting the child's success each day in a notebook, on an index card, or with some other simple and tangible marker that the child takes home to show the parents. The concrete nature of the marker offers the extra clear feedback and encouragement that some children need to stay on track and keep trying.

For Tiffany, the teacher and parents agreed that each day the child would take home one of two notes from Arlene. On days when Tiffany did well on her contract goals, she would take home the note saying "Hooray! Tiffany did her teachers' words and used friendly words and actions." On days when she didn't do so well, she would take home the note saying "Oops! Tiffany didn't do her job today. I'm hopeful she'll make better choices tomorrow."

While markers need not include any writing—sometimes they're simply a Popsicle stick with a red dot on it or a poker chip to take home and put into a jar—

Tiffany's Contract

Tiffany will show that she is a good worker by doing these jobs:

1. She will do her teachers' words.

   Examples:

   - When the teacher asks you to come to circle, you will come right away.

   - When a teacher reminds you to do your job, you will stop what you're doing and do your job.

   - Tiffany's example:

     picking up at choice time

2. She will use friendly words and actions to share space and materials.

   Examples:

   - When a classmate comes to sit near you at circle or stand near you in line, you will use friendly words and actions to share the space.

   - You will use friendly words and actions to solve problems with classmates. If your words and actions don't work, you will politely ask a teacher for help.

   - Tiffany's example:

     ① sharing in the housekeeping corner at choice time.

     ② sharing snack – pass the bowl

I understand what my good worker jobs are every day.

Tiffany
_____
Student's signature

We will help Tiffany to do her jobs, and we will celebrate with her when she does.

Justine
_____
Parent's signature

Mrs. Flye ☺
_____
Teacher's signature

in Tiffany's case the notes from Arlene were a way to emphasize the positive. The "Hooray" note restated the positive habits that the child was developing, and the "Oops" note matter-of-factly expressed faith in the child's ability to do better the next day.

Frequent reminders to the child from the teacher

Even with a contract in place and a tangible marker to take home each day, children often do better when they have regular reminders and encouragement for the particular goals they're working on. Teachers might take a moment each morning to briefly role play the expected behaviors with the child—for example, how to ask to borrow something in a friendly way or what to do if the teacher says to stop an activity before you're done. Throughout the day, brief feedback and reminders can help the child stay on track. For example, Arlene would say, "Tiffany, I noticed you came right to circle when I asked you to" or "Tiffany, I noticed you didn't come to circle right away at Morning Meeting. Try coming right away when I ask you to after Academic Choice."

A simple way to evaluate each day's success

It's important to choose a simple, clear way to evaluate whether the child met the goals each day. For Tiffany, Arlene made a checklist of seven blocks of time when Tiffany's behavior would be observed: Morning Meeting, group reading time, snack time, during the Academic Choice activity, recess and lunch, math block, and time for getting ready to go home. Tiffany had to meet her goals of "doing the teachers' words" and "using friendly words and actions" in five out of the seven time blocks to get the "Hooray" note that day. At the end of each day, Arlene would have a brief conversation with Tiffany—always out of earshot of the other children—to go over the day's checklist and determine together which note should go home that day.

Whether or not the child met the goals that day, a matter-of-fact reaction from the teacher is all that's needed. "You got six check marks today," the teacher might say on a good day. On a bad day, a simple "I know you can do better tomorrow" will do. Gushing over accomplishments or lecturing about mistakes can make matters worse.

A celebration of achievement

While the emphasis in using contracts is on helping children develop internal control, many teachers find that external celebrations along the way are often a necessary impetus for children to change behavioral habits. A key element of the contract, therefore, is that after the student has brought home a certain number of "good day" markers, the achievement is marked with a family celebration.

Teachers who have used contracts successfully agree that the most effective celebrations are modest: the chance to play a special game with a parent, a visit to a favorite place, or even a special responsibility such as taking a class pet home over the weekend.

How many "good day" markers a child has to get before celebrating depends on the age and needs of the child, says Charney. "We want to provide a tension between what is going to stretch the student and what is realistic," she writes (Charney 2002, 353). "If the number is too high, the child becomes discouraged. If it is too low, it becomes a joke." For older students, the bar is often set higher than for younger students.

Spotlight: An Individual Contract

In Tiffany's case, the parents decided that there should be a celebration every day that the child brings home a "Hooray" note. Arlene suggested that the celebrations be kept simple so they'll be do-able, and so they wouldn't become more important than the goals Tiffany is working on.

Tiffany's parents then decided that some appropriate celebrations might be for the child to have an extra story at bedtime, to play a board game with them, and to make cookies with them to bring to school. Tiffany herself suggested that she could be allowed to take a guided reading book home—"even when it's not my turn"—to read to her mom.

Starting a contract

Once the teacher feels that a contract might help a child, s/he meets with the parents to discuss the idea. If the adults are in agreement, the child is invited in to talk about how the contract will work. The student, the parents, and the teacher all sign the contract, and the contract is put into action.

Exactly how the teacher contacts the parents and meets with them varies. Here's how Arlene did it:

An inviting phone call

Arlene's first step was to call Tiffany's parents. "I have an idea," she said, "that I think will help Tiffany to remember her jobs in the classroom and will help you know what's going on at school. Could we get together tomorrow at 9:30 when the kids are at gym?"

It's important to know that Arlene and the family had already built a positive relationship. During the first week of school, Arlene had called every family in the class to report something their child did—something as simple as "Leo really enjoyed playing in the sandbox today"—just to let them know that she noticed their child. Within the next two weeks, she made another check-in phone call to ask how parents were feeling about school and to say something positive that she noticed about their child. She sent home lots of "Kindergarten Updates," informal notes telling about classroom happenings and interesting anecdotes. "I was building rapport," Arlene explains. "If you don't do that, parents aren't going to trust you enough to work on a problem with you."

It's also important, says Arlene, that the phone call to initiate an individual contract isn't the first time the family hears about the behavior issue in question. In Tiffany's case, she let the parents know early on of Tiffany's difficulty with following directions and being friendly with classmates. And she raised the issue in subsequent conversations. The phone call offering a "new idea" and asking for a meeting, therefore, did not come as a surprise to the child's parents.

Meeting with the parents

Tiffany's mom, Justine, readily agreed to come to the meeting. At the meeting, Arlene explained that often when reminders and other strategies haven't helped a child improve his/her behavior, a contract with positive behavior goals can help. She emphasized the nonpunitive nature of contracts, described how the process usually works, and asked Justine's opinion about trying a contract with Tiffany. Justine was open to the idea, so they discussed the details. Both Justine and Arlene contributed ideas for how to evaluate Tiffany's success each day, what kind of marker to use, how often to celebrate, and how to celebrate. "It's important to give families plenty of chances to share their expertise," says Arlene.

At the same time, it can be helpful for the teacher to offer suggestions on how to allow the contract to work at its best. In that spirit, Arlene offered Justine some tips on how to respond to the notes that Tiffany would be bringing home, especially the "Oops" note. "You might try just calmly and matter-of-factly saying, 'I hope you will make better choices tomorrow. I know you can.' That's it. End of conversation," Arlene suggested. The next morning, a simple friendly reminder before the child goes off to school might be helpful, she added.

The child joins the meeting

When the class came back from gym, Arlene asked Tiffany to join the meeting. She introduced the contract and explained that it's something she and Tiffany's mom had been talking about to help her do the teacher's words and use friendly words and actions. She went through how the contract would work, then let Tiffany suggest ways to celebrate the days when she brought home a "Hooray" note.

It's important that the child sees the teacher and parent together at this meeting. "It shows the child that the school and home are cooperating and are on the same page," says Arlene. "When kids are involved in a team approach, they get the message that this is serious business."

To get Tiffany ready to use the contract, Arlene, Justine, and the child rehearsed how to do the goals stated in the contract. For example, Arlene brought an actual snack bowl to the table, and the three practiced passing the bowl around. Similarly, the group practiced using friendly words and actions when coming into a meeting circle, with the adults role playing as classmates.

Continuing with the rehearsal, Arlene asked Tiffany, "Can you think of other times when it's hard to use friendly actions and words?" The child named tines when she played in the drama corner. Arlene asked, "If Susie is wearing the dress in the drama corner and you wanted that dress, how would you handle that?" "I could say 'Let's take turns'," Tiffany answered. "Or I could play with something else until she's done."

"Inevitably, the child has all the answers," Arlene comments later. "Children just need help putting their ideas into action. The contract helps them with that."

Letting children name solutions in front of their parents can also be helpful for the parents, says Arlene. When parents see their child as a problem solver and as an individual capable of change, they're more likely to embrace the contract process.

Deciding when to end the contract

Three months into the contract, Tiffany's behavior improved dramatically, to the point where Arlene felt the contract could be discontinued. She discussed it with Tiffany's mother, and at a student-teacher-parent conference in May, all parties agreed to end the contract. Arlene continued to give verbal reminders to Tiffany, however. "I know you're not doing your contract anymore, but I know you have inside control to do your jobs," she'd tell Tiffany at the beginning of each day. At the end of each day, she'd give the child some feedback on how she did that day.

Spotlight: An Individual Contract

While Tiffany outgrew her need for a contract, some children need contracts as an ongoing support. When they're able to meet the goals of one contract consistently, other issues arise, necessitating a new contract with new goals.

Foundations of Success

Several conditions need to be true before contracts can be effective:

The teacher assumes the child wants to "be good"

The teacher believes that the child wants to be liked by teachers and classmates, to feel competent and skillful, and to fit in. As Charney writes, "Even when children retort 'I don't care,' I assume that they do care—almost all the time." (Charney 2002, 341)

The teacher expresses empathy for the child

The teacher tries to understand the child and has respect for the child's efforts. The teacher conveys a sense that s/he knows where the child is coming from and believes the child has the potential to change.

Expected behaviors have been taught

Before holding the child accountable for his/her behavior in a contract, the teacher carefully introduces, models, and allows the children to practice the expected behaviors, with reviews as needed thereafter.

The teacher and family have a relationship of trust

The teacher has let the family know often that s/he notices the child and appreciates the child as an individual. The family has come to trust that the teacher respects them and has the best interests of the child in mind.

Chapter Nine

PAYING ATTENTION TO THE LAST SIX WEEKS OF SCHOOL

he end of the year
is a time for parents, the teacher, and the child to look back and celebrate
all the hard work done during the year. It's a big part of getting the child
ready to take off to the next level, a big part of instilling
confidence in the child about the next school year.

Parent of a fifth grader

Good endings are just as important as good beginnings. We've invested time and energy in engaging parents right from the start of the school year. We've worked hard to sustain communications and relationships with them throughout the year. Now it's time to finish the year with the same thoughtful attention to parents with which we began.

The trouble is it's May and life has become very hectic. We need to finish the curriculum, conduct year-end activities, complete report cards, and wade through mounds of year-end paper work, all the while keeping the children focused on school when they seem only interested in counting down the days until summer. We ourselves are tired from the year and are looking forward to some rest and revival. Who has time or energy to work with parents at this time of year?

If we're lucky, a sane inner voice—or perhaps the voice of a colleague or mentor—tells us we can and would be wise to summon some time and energy for purposeful year-end work with parents. Many teachers know the importance of helping *students* bring a calm and thoughtful closure to their year. We create opportunities for children to reflect on and celebrate their year of learning. We try to alleviate any worries they might have about the summer or the next grade.

We take deliberate measures to help students end the year feeling confident about themselves and in positive anticipation of the coming year.

It's important to apply the same care with parents as school draws to a close. They've worked hard all year too, getting to know us and our classroom practices, helping their children with homework, noticing their victories, offering them encouragement through the tough times, staying in communication with the teacher, perhaps helping out in the classroom. The last six weeks of school is the time for teachers and parents to come together to acknowledge all that hard work and to celebrate what the children, with the parents' support, have been able to accomplish. It's a time, too, for teachers to address any worries parents may have about what the summer and the next school year will bring for their child.

Like working with parents at any other time, it is possible to keep this work manageable, even given our busy year-end schedules. Often a brief letter or a quick meeting goes a long way. This chapter will offer some suggestions for working with parents at the end of the year. The ideas aren't fancy or novel— I've found that simple, sensible, time-tested closure activities work best and are most welcomed by parents. Whether you use these ideas as is, adapt them, or spring from them to develop ideas of your own, the important thing is to treat the last weeks of school, like the first weeks of school, as a distinct time and to move with intention through them.

Goals in Working with Parents in the Last Six Weeks

Goals in
Working with
Parents in
the Last Six
Weeks

To allow parents to feel a sense of pride and accomplishment about the past year

All families—those whose children sailed through the year and those whose children struggled with every assignment—have something from the year that they can look back upon with pride. For one family, it's the child completing a complicated project with the parent's help. For another, it's the parent and child settling on a more effective homework routine. For yet another, it's the parent learning ways to help the child better handle frustration. All are noteworthy accomplishments. As teachers, we can provide families with opportunities to recognize and celebrate these sources of pride.

To help prepare parents for the summer

The end of school can bring mixed emotions for some children. While summer may mean no homework and more free time for months, for some children it may also mean the end of some friendships or the loss of a safe place to go each day. Teachers can suggest ways for parents to help their children cope with any sadness or anxiety about the end of school. Meanwhile, as the end of the year approaches, many parents have worries of their own. Chief among them may be the concern that over the summer their children will lose everything they learned during the year. Teachers can help on this front as well by giving parents practical ideas for minimizing this "summer learning loss."

To help families look ahead to the next school year

While students wonder or worry about their next grade, their parents may be having similar concerns: "Who will be my child's new teacher and classmates next year?" "Will my son like school as much as he did this year?" "What will the schoolwork be like?" "Will the teacher understand him and our family?" Often, having information helps parents feel more reassured. Teachers can tell parents as much as they know about the coming year—what the next grade's curriculum consists of, what school-wide activities are planned, who the next grade's teachers are, and so forth. In addition, teachers can let parents know what's being done in class to inform and reassure students about their next grade. When parents know that their children are prepared and feeling positive about moving up, their own worries are more likely to subside.

Chapter Nine

Practical Ideas

Here are some ideas for helping parents celebrate the year's accomplishments, prepare for the summer, and get ready for the next school year:

Celebrating the year's accomplishments

Hold a one-on-one meeting with each parent

Many teachers use part of the last parent-teacher conference of the year to do a broad whole-year reflection. The parent and teacher together review the child's portfolio, compare accomplishments with goals, note special areas of growth, and look forward to the year ahead. If this last conference is to take place weeks or months before school ends, however, teachers may want to schedule separate reflection conferences with parents that truly take place at the end of the year. (For an example, see "Reflecting on September's Hopes and Dreams" on page 190.)

Create a "museum" of proud work from the year

Some teachers set up a special year-end open house for parents to see a display of the children's learning from the year. One way to do this is to have students look through their year-long portfolios, choose samples that illustrate areas in which they have shown the most growth, and arrange a display of these items on their desk. During the open house, parents walk around this "museum," admiring the children's work while each child talks about the significance of what s/he has chosen to display. Around the room might be additional samples of students' work, perhaps products of group efforts.

As students lead their parents on a tour of the museum, the teacher can circulate the room, talking with individual parents, noting the special efforts they made to support their child during the year. It's a time to congratulate parents on a specific achievement or relish with them a special memory from the year.

**Practical
Ideas**

Share "What We Learned" lists with parents

In many classrooms, students brainstorm all the things they learned during the year, listing or drawing them on big sheets of paper that are then displayed in the room. Younger children might attach a page of "hard math," list words they can spell, or draw pictures about the science projects they did over the year. Older children might list all fifty state names and capitals, show off fancy technical terms in science, or give examples of hard math equations they solved. These displays clearly make students feel proud, smart, and confident about themselves as learners.

They can also encourage a sense of accomplishment and optimism in parents. Teachers can invite parents to drop in to the classroom to see these lists, display them at year-end open houses, or type up their contents for inclusion in a classroom newsletter or a letter sent home.

Preparing for the summer

Send a group year-end letter

An efficient way to communicate with parents about the summer might be to send a letter home or to write about the topic in the class newsletter. In both cases, here are some points to remember:

- Empathize with parents' concern about "summer learning loss" and offer practical ideas for minimizing it.

Be Specific in Acknowledging Parents' Efforts

Whether you're writing a note to parents, talking to them in person during a meeting, or chatting with them during a year-end open house, it's best to be specific when acknowledging their support of their children's learning during the year. Some examples:

"Lawrence made so much progress in reading partly because you spent each night sitting and reading with him."

"Ellie was able to make so much progress in writing because you made it fun for her to practice at home. Helping her keep a journal of day-to-day events made a huge difference."

"Maggie was able to make such strides in her organizational skills because you helped her use a checklist to get ready for school each day."

If you'll be walking around an open house to offer these comments to parents, you may want to prepare ahead of time what to say to each parent. Jot down a few key words for each family. Keep the list handy to glance at as you mill about the room.

Chapter Nine

- Encourage parents to keep summer learning fun and avoid having it become a chore.

- Remind parents that the end of the school year can cause anxiety for some children.

- Encourage parents to show empathy for their child's worries about the summer and to encourage the child to talk about them.

Communicate through conferences or report cards

Teachers can also talk with parents about the summer at year-end conferences or in the narratives that they write on the children's report cards. This allows for tailoring the comments to suit each individual child. Just as we urge parents not to overdo their efforts to keep their child learning over the summer, it's important that we not overwhelm parents with suggestions. Try to focus on just one or two of the most important things for the child to keep working on or for the parent to do, and keep the tone positive. Here are some examples:

"Charlene might enjoy and benefit from regularly reading with you this summer—perhaps fifteen minutes each evening or most evenings."

"Andrew enjoyed making fruit salad so much in class. You might try to get him cooking with you this summer. Encourage him to read and follow recipes as a way to practice math and reading."

"Morgan seems a little sad about leaving the classroom and his classmates. Bringing up the topic and giving him a chance to talk about it might help. You could also help him stay in touch with a few classmates over the summer."

Looking ahead to the next school year

Practical Ideas

Tell parents about "step-up" activities in class

Many teachers structure step-up activities that help students learn about and look forward to the next grade with confidence. The class might write their questions about the next grade for students in that grade to answer. Students might be paired with someone in the older grade so the two can spend some time talking. There might be a "step-up day" when children visit a classroom one grade up. Or teachers of the older grade might be invited to come meet the younger children and answer questions. It benefits parents to hear about all these activities. Knowing that their children's worries are being addressed at school can help parents feel more at ease.

Teachers can tell parents about these activities in a brief letter or the class newsletter. I often use the "Ask me about…" newsletter format for this purpose. (See Chapter 4 for more about these newsletters.) By allowing the child to do much of the explaining, this format can, in some cases, show parents that the child is more at ease about moving into the new grade than they thought. More importantly, it can foster meaningful parent-child conversations about an important school topic.

A sample is on the opposite page.

Arrange for parents to meet next year's teacher

Parents often feel more reassured about the coming year after meeting their child's new teacher. The school's last open house of the year can be a good time for these meetings. If you already know which teachers your students will have, ask those teachers if they would be willing to have their next year's parents visit

---

Looking Ahead to Next Year

As the school year comes to an end, many children may feel anxious about what lies ahead. You can help by talking with your child about it often, sharing similar worries you may have had as a child, and talking about worries you may now have about starting something new.

We are having discussions and doing activities in class to help children prepare for the summer and the next school year. Talk with your child about these. You can use the questions below as conversation starters.

Please let me know if I can be of any help at school.

Ask me about...

- What kind of homework I will have in fourth grade

- One thing that I'm looking forward to in fourth grade

- What my daily schedule will be like in fourth grade

- What I learned about the teachers in fourth grade

- What questions I still have about fourth grade

Chapter Nine

for a portion of the evening. If you don't yet know which teachers your students will have, parents can visit all or some of the teachers of that grade to get a general sense of that grade level's staff.

Tell parents about developmental changes to expect in their children

As described in Chapter 3, it's important for teachers to talk with parents about children's developmental stages. The end of the year is a key time for this. As school draws to a close, I give parents a handout that outlines the physical, social, language, and cognitive developmental traits that are widely seen in children one year older than their child is now. This prepares parents for the changes they are likely to encounter in the coming year and gives them ideas for how best to support their children through the new school year.

Spotlight:

Reflecting on September's Hopes and Dreams

Second Grade
Rolling Hills Elementary School
Holland, Pennsylvania

**Spotlight:
Reflecting on
September's
Hopes and
Dreams**

It's a warm afternoon in June. In a classroom at Rolling Hills Elementary School in Holland, Pennsylvania, second grade teacher Barb Del Nero is sitting with a student's parent. The two are re-reading the hopes and dreams the parent named for her child back in September: "I want her to be a better reader and get faster at math." The parent smiles a little reading that. Teacher and parent then leaf through a binder of some of the child's work from the year—math puzzles done, stories and poems created, drawings made as part of science projects, papers from literature circle. There are murmurs from both adults: "Oh, I remember that assignment," "She struggled over that one," and "I was so proud of her when she wrote that poem."

Barb then engages the parent in reflecting on the child's accomplishments in the areas named in the parent's hopes and dreams. "What do you see that Brianna accomplished this year in improving her reading and math?" Barb asks. Brianna's mom thinks for a moment, then begins pointing out growths she's noticed, occasionally referring back to her daughter's work.

This scene is repeated with every family during the last two weeks of school in Barb's class. It's the logical end of the goal-setting process that she and other teachers at her school use with parents. At the beginning of the year she listens to parents' hopes and dreams for their child for the year. In January she asks whether parents think the hopes and dreams should be revised given the child's progress. Then, in June she listens to parents' feelings about how well those hopes and dreams were realized.

"That meeting made such a difference," says Brooke Holdsman, whose son Abbott was in Barb's class. "At the end of the year, what's on parents' minds is obviously what progress their children made." That progress is sometimes hard to see in the midst of the busy daily life of school. The year-end meeting, Brooke says, gives parents a chance to stop, step back, and assess just what the child did accomplish.

Sure, report cards during the year also inform families, but, Barb points out, "Unlike report cards, the focus in these meetings is on what the *parents* wanted for their child and how the *parents* think their child did in those areas."

A celebration of growth

Often, parents think their children did pretty well, and the meetings are a recognition and a celebration. One parent wanted her child to become a better reader. "Now she reads in bed and doesn't want to turn the light out," she told Barb.

Another student had a lot of anxiety about a particular classmate with whom he would be attending a special program that year. The goal his mother named was for him to get along better with that classmate. At the year-end conference, the parent said to Barb, "After a while, my son could sleep better at night because he wasn't worrying about what's going to happen with Michael the next morning."

"I would come out of the conferences with such gratitude," says Barb, because "as a teacher, you don't realize what you've accomplished with the students sometimes until a parent reflects it back to you. Without these end-of-the-year conferences, I might not hear these things from parents."

Other times, the parents' goals were not achieved or were only partly achieved. The conference then becomes a time to reflect on this together and come up with ideas that might help the child in that area over the summer and into the following year. It can also be a time for teachers to point out the areas in which the student did make significant progress.

Comparing different views

Sometimes a parent and the teacher have different views about a student's progress. The conference then is a chance to compare thoughts and, in the best of cases, reach a clearer understanding of the child's growth.

For example, Brooke, who at the beginning of the year had hoped her son Abbott would get better at pulling his thoughts together into writing, felt that Abbott improved only somewhat in that area. Barb, on the other hand, felt he improved a lot. "When she said that I laughed a little and didn't believe her," recalls Brooke. But after a while she saw that while she was basing her conclusion largely on the writing that Abbott did at home, Barb was basing hers also on Abbott's school writing. For a number of possible reasons—perhaps Abbott was tired after a whole day of school, perhaps his mind was pulled toward other things at home—his home writing was less successful than his school writing.

In addition, while Brooke was looking for examples of beautiful finished writing, Barb looked more for incremental changes from one piece of writing to the next, changes that are the building blocks of producing beautiful finished pieces. The conversation helped both the teacher and the parent understand this about each other. Ultimately, says Brooke, after considering Abbott's school writings and hearing the teacher explain the importance of the incremental changes, she walked away more reassured about her son's writing ability.

Looking ahead to the summer and beyond

The year-end meetings are also a chance for the parents and the teacher to think ahead about the summer and the following school year. Some families want to brainstorm summer strategies that might help their child retain the growth they made during the year. Others want to know what challenges await their child in the fall, what new skills s/he might be learning. In schools where the teacher has input into students' class placement for the fall, the meetings are also a chance for the teacher to hear parents' thoughts in this area.

Tips for year-end conferences

Spotlight:
Reflecting on
September's
Hopes and
Dreams

Schedule sensibly

While it's important to give each family enough time, it's also easy for teachers to overextend themselves, Barb says. She has found that a sensible balance is to schedule twenty to thirty minutes with each parent, and no more than two conferences in the morning before school and two in the afternoon after school. This allows her to see all parents in about two weeks. Teachers who want to have fewer conferences per day could stretch the schedule out over a month.

Invite parents to choose their time

Parents are more likely to show up if they're able to choose appointment times that work for them. Just as with the hopes and dreams conferences at the beginning of the year, Barb's invitation letter asks parents to name their preferred day and time during the next couple of weeks, either just before school or just after school. If a parent still doesn't make it to a conference, Barb mails the parent's hopes and dreams and the child's binder home, along with a note inviting the parent to reflect on the child's progress in realizing those hopes and dreams.

Keep careful documentation

These year-end conferences work best when parents have their hopes and dreams for their child—either the September ones or the revised January ones—and their child's work from the year right there to look at, says Barb. She creates a binder for each child. Into the binder go the parents' hopes and dreams form, along with samples of the child's school work and any individual education plan paperwork.

A special time for looking back and looking ahead

The last weeks of school are a special time for looking back and looking ahead. When teachers close the year with care, as through these year-end meetings, they acknowledge the hard work that they and parents did together. They honor the relationships built. When teachers look with parents at what's coming around the bend, they help ensure that parents stay invested in their child's journey of learning.

**Chapter
Nine**

Appendix A

Morning Meeting Begins at 7:15 PM!

Ideas for using this familiar classroom routine at back-to-school nights, open houses, and other parent meetings

By Pamela Porter

The following first appeared in the Summer 2003 issue of the *Responsive Classroom® Newsletter* published by Northeast Foundation for Children.

It's back-to-school night at Flanders Elementary School in East Lyme, Connecticut. As parents and guardians arrive at Andy Dousis's fourth grade classroom, he welcomes them warmly and invites them to read the "Morning Message" chart that is addressed to them.

September 23

Welcome Families and Friends,

Please come in and make a name tag. Take a look around the room. Then find one person you don't know well and introduce yourself.

On the chart, please write one question or comment you have about what your child will be doing this year.

We will begin at 7:15.

Mr. Dousis

Once most of the adults have arrived and have had a chance to make name tags and introduce themselves to someone, Mr. Dousis rings a chime to get the group's attention. "It's time to come to meeting," he says, and invites everyone to find a seat in a large circle of chairs he has arranged for them.

"I'm Andy Dousis, your student's teacher," he begins. "Thank you for coming. Tonight I want to share some of the things we'll be learning in school this year and to give us all a chance to get to know each other a little better. We start every day in this classroom with a twenty-minute Morning Meeting. Tonight we'll do our own version of a Morning Meeting so you can experience firsthand what this meeting is like."

Teachers using the *Responsive Classroom* approach often structure family nights using a Morning Meeting format. (See box on page 199 for sources of information on Morning Meeting.) This sets a positive tone for the evening, helps adults to feel welcomed and included, and gives families a firsthand experience of something their children do every day at school.

Morning Meeting Begins at 7:15 PM!

Whether it's "back-to-school" night or one of the curriculum meetings her school holds each year for parents and guardians, Sarah Magee, a special education teacher at Regional Multicultural Magnet School in New London, Connecticut, says she always begins these evenings in a circle using a Morning Meeting format.

"It helps develop positive community relationships," she notes, "and it lets families experience something their children take part in every day. After adults go through a Morning Meeting, they come to understand the importance of teaching social skills and they see how academic and social learning are woven together during this part of the day."

Goals for the meeting

When teachers ask for guidance in planning a Morning Meeting for parents and guardians, I suggest they begin by keeping the following two goals in mind:

1. To foster a sense of community and help people get to know each other

One important goal for these evenings is to set a friendly, welcoming tone that helps people feel at ease and included as members of the school community. We know that when children feel like they belong, they participate in more meaningful ways. This is true for adults as well. Teachers report that when parents/guardians know and feel comfortable with the school staff and with one another, they are more likely to get their children together outside of school, volunteer, participate actively in the life of the school, and seek help for their children when it's needed.

2. To share information about the classroom and curriculum in ways that are interactive, meaningful, and fun

The meeting can be used as an effective starting point for sharing information about the curriculum and events in the classroom. But more importantly, when parents/guardians experience a Morning Meeting—exchanging greetings, learning each other's names, engaging in an activity together—they see for themselves the powerful social and academic learning that is happening during this time and the value of taking time to build a sense of classroom community.

Guidelines for leading a Morning Meeting with parents

One of the most important things to keep in mind is that some adults may feel awkward and unsure of what to do when they first enter the classroom. They may feel they have already taken a big risk in just coming for the meeting. Be sure to greet people at the door when they arrive. Provide name tags so people can learn and become comfortable using each other's names. And have a message chart and a meeting circle ready and waiting for them.

Once the adults are gathered in the circle, introduce the meeting. It is usually sufficient to say that the students begin every day with a Morning Meeting—a fifteen- to twenty-minute routine that builds community, sets a positive tone for the day, nurtures confidence and excitement about learning, and improves academic and social skills—and that tonight the adults will have a chance to experience a Morning Meeting firsthand. Below are some additional guidelines for making the meeting successful.

Choose low-risk activities that help people get to know each other or that connect with the curriculum

Especially at the beginning of the year, avoid greetings and activities that are too silly or require physical contact. It's also important to avoid activities that could embarrass anyone or put an individual on the spot. A greeting in which two adults are partnered and then introduce each other to the group often works well: "This is Magda and her son is Issac. He loves basketball."

Group activities that work well in this setting include "A Warm Wind Blows" and "I'm Thinking of a Number Between 1 and 100." Both activities keep the focus on the group as a whole and are easy to teach and fun to play. (Instructions for many Morning Meeting activities are available on the *Responsive Classroom* website, www.responsiveclassroom.org.)

You may also ask students for suggestions of an appropriate activity for their families. Family members often enjoy learning a favorite activity of the students.

If you include sharing, keep it brief and focused. For example, you might ask people to share the names and grades of their children or one thing their child likes to do. A round robin format lets everyone say something (or pass) but does not require questions and comments. This saves time and avoids the lengthy introduction and teaching that other forms of sharing require.

Bring the message chart into the circle and use it to launch into the discussion of curriculum

Morning Meeting Begins at 7:15 PM!

Just as it's used in the classroom, the message chart can be used to shift the focus to the topic at hand. For example, the question on the chart might be, "Write one question you have about what your child will be doing this year." Reading the parents/guardians' questions provides a nice segue into the topic for the evening.

Teachers may also want to share a sample of a Morning Message chart from the classroom. Through looking at a chart that the students and teacher have already worked with, the group will see the wide range of academic skills addressed in this component of Morning Meeting.

Before moving on to the topic for the evening, take a few minutes to reflect together on the meeting

After everyone has experienced the meeting, it can be valuable to ask them to reflect briefly on the experience. Some simple questions that work well are:

- How do you feel now compared to when you first entered the room?

- What social skills did we practice in the meeting? What academic skills?

- What are some of the ways Morning Meeting might help children feel comfortable, confident, and ready for learning?

Follow up with written information about Morning Meeting

Because there will always be family members who cannot attend school gatherings, it's a good idea to have written information about Morning Meeting and other topics addressed that can be sent to families.

Some teachers also follow up with regular newsletters to families. Along with updates about what's going on in math, writing, science, and social studies, fourth grade teacher Mike Anderson includes a section on Morning Meeting in his weekly newsletter. Here's one example:

"This week during the Sharing portion of our meeting, we're continuing to work on creating a good lead for narrative writing. We've also enjoyed using the Group Activity time to reenact scenes from the book I'm reading aloud. In addition to helping students learn to cooperate and work as a team, this activity has strengthened students' comprehension of key scenes of the book."

The benefits are multifold

Since Andy Dousis began holding Morning Meetings with families several years ago, he's noticed a significant difference in his relationship with families. "Before, they used to question the value of Morning Meeting a lot. Now, more often than not, they want to tell me how much they appreciate what the students are learning in this daily routine—the social skills and the academic skills. Family involvement has also improved dramatically since I began using this structure for open houses. Now when I ask families for help with anything, they're there."

Appendix A

Resources on Morning Meeting

The Morning Meeting Book by Roxann Kriete with contributions by Lynn Bechtel. Northeast Foundation for Children, 2002.

"Morning Meeting: A Powerful Way to Begin the Day" in *Responsive Classroom Newsletter,* Winter 1999.
www.responsiveclassroom.org/11_1NL_1.htm

"The Power of Morning Meeting: 'Like Being at the Breakfast Table'" in *Responsive Classroom Newsletter,* Fall 2001.
www.responsiveclassroom.org/13_4NL_1.htm

Appendix B

Wonderful Wednesdays

Inviting parents into our classroom community

By Caltha Crowe

The following first appeared in the Fall 2004 issue of the *Responsive Classroom® Newsletter* published by Northeast Foundation for Children.

Morning Meeting is over and writing workshop is underway. The children are scattered around the room sketching and then writing about objects that "called out to them." Erin's dad is leaning against the file cabinet, absorbed as he sketches a ceramic rooster. Lauren's mom is quietly bouncing baby Amy on her knee as she writes down her thoughts.

I ring the chime, signaling the group to come to the rug for group sharing. We go around the circle, and everyone who wants to reads a favorite line from his/her writing. Erin's dad, Phil, says, "Thank you for inviting me to be part of this beautiful morning. Here's something I wrote: 'The rooster crows, its feathers glowing red, yellow, and blue against the alabaster egg.'" Phil, an artist, was never comfortable in school. Today, his relaxed and engaged participation in the sketching, writing, and sharing indicates a newfound easiness with school and hints at a beginning understanding of the power that such activities have in deepening his daughter's learning.

For a number of years now I've invited parents into my classroom for these weekly or biweekly open houses, which we call Wonderful Wednesdays. I keep these days structured around workshop-type activities and ask parents to join us as full participants. They're not there to be helpers or passive observers. They aren't there to see a show or to be the show. Rather, the purpose is for parents to experience day-to-day life in our classroom in a safe and comfortable way.

Helping parents understand today's classroom

Classrooms today are often so different from those of a generation ago. When most of my students' parents think of reading, writing, spelling, and math, they probably don't picture the workshop setting, or practice through games and fun, or choice in academic activities—all of which are routine parts of their children's school day. An important goal of Wonderful Wednesdays, then, is to allow parents to understand these approaches by participating in them, by laughing with us and thinking hard with us, by experiencing that delicate balance of low stress and high rigor that we achieve at our best moments.

One Wednesday, Gretchen's mom came. Gretchen is a precocious child with exceptional number sense. Her mother had said to me that she was sure our math program wasn't challenging enough for her daughter. That day, the children brainstormed ideas for math choice and then set off to do their chosen activities. Gretchen, a classmate Katie, and their two moms were soon engrossed in a game of Target. As they finished the game, Gretchen's mom said, "I really had to think." I believe she got a glimpse of how school is both fun and rigorous, and of how her daughter is allowed to work at the appropriate level of challenge for her.

Wonderful Wednesdays

A way for me to get to know parents

The school-home connection is a two-way street. It's just as important for me to know parents as it is for parents to know our classroom and my teaching approach. I teach in a large school in a busy community where it can be hard to establish tight connections with families. Even so, I think that through Wonderful Wednesdays, I have been able to attain a measure of familiarity and rapport with many of them. This connection not only makes my work more enjoyable, but it is essential to my work, for in order to teach my students well, I need to know something of their life outside of school.

For example, Mike's writing is full of creative ideas but equally full of spelling and punctuation mistakes. His older brother, Toby, who was in my class last year, worried over every detail of his writing and produced polished, clean pieces. As I watch their mother, Lynne, in our classroom, I see that she is more like Toby, something of a perfectionist. When Lynne responds to a letter that Mike writes to her by covering it with red marks, I am able to keep the family picture in mind and avoid becoming irritated with Lynne. I set up a conference with her to discuss ways that we can collaborate to help Mike develop his unique talents as well as help him meet minimum standards for clean writing.

Relaxed participation, realistic view

Since Wonderful Wednesdays go on for most of the year, and parents can come as few or as many times as they'd like, there's usually only a small number of parents in the classroom on any given Wednesday.

Moreover, Wonderful Wednesdays are drop-in events. I don't ask parents to tell me ahead of time when they're coming. Some take the afternoon off from work or other commitments. Others stop by during their lunch hour. Some come by for Morning Meeting before they head off for their day. Whether or not we have parents join us, whether they stay for ten minutes or two hours, the class goes on with its day as usual, and any parents present simply join in the activities.

All this means that the parents, the children, and I can all get to know each other and learn with each other in a more relaxed way than at formal gatherings such as conferences or back-to-school night. Parents also get a more realistic feel for what it's like to be a student in our classroom.

A foundation for further cooperation

The rewards of involving parents through Wonderful Wednesdays pay off all year long. Ray is a student who has trouble controlling his body. The other children avoid him, afraid that his rough movements will hurt them. When I discuss this with Ray's mother, our conversation goes more smoothly because of a level of trust that we have built through our contact on several Wonderful Wednesdays. She knows that I like Ray and that our community is a safe place where Ray feels like he belongs. She tells me she's eager to work with me to help Ray learn to control his body and be more accepted by his classmates.

Start small, then build

Teachers who want to try something like Wonderful Wednesdays might want to start small, maybe doing it just once. If the event is a success, do it again. Then add more days until having parents learning alongside their children becomes a regular feature of your classroom. (See the next page for more tips.)

Wonderful Wednesdays

Tips for Success

Wait until the classroom community feels solid before starting

This might be around October or November. The goal is for parents to feel the power of a caring and rigorous learning environment, a goal best achieved once the community is strong.

Announce dates for the year in the initial invitation

The dates, even if they're tentative, allow parents to plan ahead

Maintain a predictable schedule on Wonderful Wednesdays

For example, in our class, math Academic Choice is at 10:15 every Wonderful Wednesday, and the Cherry Pie spelling game is always at 12:45. I include the schedule in the initial invitation. Parents can then join us for a subject that they feel comfortable with.

Plan activities that exemplify community-oriented education

Because a goal is to help parents understand our class's emphasis on cooperative learning, I save math quizzes and even guided reading groups for another day.

Clearly ask that parents participate

I say, "Join us as frequently or as infrequently as you please. All we ask is that you join us as a participant in our activities."

Explain that no parent has to perform

I'm careful to explain that participating is not the same as performing, and that no one is expected to perform. I tell parents, for example, that they might read their own book alongside their child, but they won't be asked to read it aloud in front of the class.

Don't do Wonderful Wednesdays on days with "specials"

Wonderful Wednesdays don't include music, PE, or other specials. It just doesn't feel collegial to announce to my colleagues that some of my students' parents will be joining their class every other Wednesday. Wonderful Wednesdays include time in our classroom only.

Here's the invitation that Caltha sends to parents:

Please join us for:

Wonderful Wednesdays

Join the Community of Bookmunching Eagles for all or any part of the day.
Join us as frequently or as infrequently as you please.
All we ask is that you join us as a participant in our activities.

Our first event will be
Wednesday, November 3, 2004

Our schedule:

9:15–9:40	Morning Meeting
10:15–11:00	math games (Come prepared to join in.)
11:00–12:00	reader's workshop (Bring your own book to read.)
12:00–12:45	artist/writer's workshop (Bring a notebook and be prepared to write.)
12:45	spelling games (Play a round of the famous "Cherry Pie.")
1:50	read-aloud (Listen to a great picture book.)
2:10–3:00	science/social studies workshop (This may get messy. Be prepared to join in.)

Tentative future dates: November 17, December 1, December 15, January 12, January 26, February 23, March 9, March 23, March 30, April 13, May 4, May 18, June 1, June 15

This is a drop-in event. RSVP is unnecessary. Ms. Crowe

Appendix C

Letter to Parents about the *Responsive Classroom®* Approach

Below is a sample letter giving parents an overview of the *Responsive Classroom* approach. You may want to shorten it or adapt it in other ways to suit your needs.

[Date]

Dear Parents,

I want to let you know of an approach to teaching that I use. It's called the **Responsive Classroom®** approach. It's been used success-fully by elementary teachers in schools around the country for over twenty years to create learning environments where children thrive academically, socially, and emotionally.

The **Responsive Classroom** approach was developed by classroom teachers. It emphasizes teaching children to take care of themselves, each other, and the school environment so that everyone can learn at his/her best. You'll notice our class paying attention to how students treat one another throughout the day. You'll also see a strong emphasis on students setting goals for their own learning and taking responsibil-ity for reaching those goals.

Guiding principles

The **Responsive Classroom** approach is based on theories of how children learn and on the experiences of classroom teachers. There are seven basic principles behind this approach:

- Learning social skills is as important as learning academic skills.

- How children learn is as important as what they learn: Process and content go hand in hand.

**Letter to
Parents
about the
*Responsive
Classroom*®
Approach**

- Children gain knowledge most effectively through social interaction.

- To be successful academically and socially, children need to learn cooperation, assertion, responsibility, empathy, and self-control.

- Knowing the children we teach—individually, culturally, and developmentally—is as important as knowing the content we teach.

- Knowing the families of the children we teach and inviting their participation is essential to children's education.

- How the adults at school work together is as important as how skillful each individual teacher is: Lasting change begins with the adult community.

Teaching practices

The **Responsive Classroom** approach includes the following main parts. We will be using some or all of these in our classroom this year.

Morning Meeting ■ gathering as a whole class each morning to greet one another, share news, and warm up for the day ahead

Rule Creation ■ helping students create classroom rules to ensure an environment that allows all class members to meet their learning goals

Interactive Modeling ■ teaching children expected behaviors through a unique modeling technique

Positive Teacher Language ■ using words and tone in ways that promote children's active learning, sense of community, and self-discipline

Strategies for Stopping Misbehavior ■ stopping misbehavior quickly and respectfully so that positive behaviors are restored

Guided Discovery ■ introducing classroom materials using a format that encourages independence, creativity, and responsibility

Academic Choice ■ increasing student learning by allowing students teacher-structured choices in their work

Classroom Organization ■ setting up the physical room in ways that encourage students' independence, cooperation, and productivity

Working with Families ■ creating avenues for hearing parents' insights and helping them understand the school's teaching approaches

Collaborative Problem-Solving ■ using conferencing, role-playing, and other strategies to resolve problems with students

Appendix C

Please let me know if you have any questions. You can also learn more about the **Responsive Classroom** approach by contacting the developers of the approach at www.responsiveclassroom.org or 800-360-6332.

I look forward to a productive and joyful year with your child!

Sincerely,

[Teacher's name]

Appendix D

Teacher-Child Problem Solving Conferences

*Involving children in finding solutions
to their behavior problems*

An adapted excerpt from *Teaching Children to Care* by Ruth Sidney Charney,
published by Northeast Foundation for Children, 2002. The following
first appeared in the Fall 2004 issue of the *Responsive Classroom®
Newsletter* published by Northeast Foundation for Children.

Derek was a fifth grader who was avoiding writing. Whenever we had writing
time, he would ask to go to the bathroom, and there he would linger. After observing this for a week, I decided to have a problem solving conference with him.

Appendix D

A problem solving conference is a technique for addressing a specific problem that a child is having. What makes it powerful is that it invites the child
into a conversation and asks for the child's take on the situation. It begins with
the teacher noticing the child's moods, actions, and interactions before helping
the child come up with possible solutions. Conducted in a nonjudgmental way,
the conference sets behavioral boundaries while giving children the opportunity
for autonomous thinking.

Below are the basic steps that I went through in the conference with Derek.
These steps are intended as guidelines to be adjusted to fit different situations.
Some conferences take five minutes; others are spread out over several days. In
some cases a conference leads to an immediate solution; in others the teacher and
child need to revisit the issue several times.

One thing that is true of all problem solving conferences, though, is that
I always hold them away from the eyes and ears of the child's classmates. It's
important that the student has privacy for these talks, and that both the teacher
and child can focus on the conversation without interruptions.

Step 1. Establishing what the teacher and student notice

A problem solving conference begins with the teacher saying positive things s/he has
noticed about the student—the student's interests, efforts, and goings-on. When we
tell students we noticed what they've done well, we begin to establish a supportive
connection, an essential step before talking about a behavior that isn't working.

With Derek, I began by saying, "I notice that you've had good ideas when we've brainstormed what we could write about. I also notice you pay attention and make helpful comments when kids share about their writing." I try to be specific in my noticings, and I name the *what*, not the *why*, of behaviors.

Next I say what behavior I've noticed that isn't working well. Here again, it's important to name specific, observable behaviors. I don't make judgments, interpret, or label. I simply describe, using a matter-of-fact tone.

"I notice that every writing time, you have to go to the bathroom," I said to Derek. I was careful not to say, "You want to avoid writing, so you say you have to go to the bathroom."

By naming the behaviors rather than interpreting them, I open the door for children to take note of their actions and offer their own interpretation. They are then more likely to take responsibility for their behavior.

After I say what I notice, I ask for the child's observations. I say simply, "What do you notice?" in a neutral tone.

When I posed this question to Derek, he said, "I just have to go to the bathroom a lot."

"So you also notice that writing has become a bathroom time for you?"

"Yeah."

Derek was agreeing with my observation. If he had disagreed, I might have said, "Well, I notice that you want to go to the bathroom at every writing time. You notice that it's only sometimes. Maybe we should both notice extra hard for the next few days and then come back and compare." I would have made a plan with Derek for how to remember our observations. But I also would have continued with the conference. It's possible to proceed in addressing a problem while we continue to gather data.

Step 2. Naming the problem and the need to solve it

The next step is to help the child see why her/his behavior is a problem and to establish that the child wants to work with the teacher to solve it.

To Derek I said, "When you go to the bathroom every writing period, you lose important work time. By the time you get back, you have to hurry and often you only get about a sentence written."

"Yeah. There's not enough time."

"So your story doesn't get very far. For example, you don't have very much yet of the story you're writing now."

"Yeah. I only have the first page."

"I want you to be able to write complete stories that you can be proud of. So this seems like a problem we should work on. What do you think?"

"I guess so."

Here it's important for the teacher to express positive intent—for the student to get along with others, have friends, enjoy and take pride in his/her work, solve math word problems, or follow directions—and to show faith that the child will make progress.

Sometimes when we ask whether a child wants to work with us on the problem, we get only a slight nod or other gesture of agreement—which is fine. We go ahead. Other times, a child refuses adamantly: "No, I don't need help!" or "No, I don't think it's a problem." If this happens, it might be useless to push ahead with the conference. However, it's important that I state the expectations for behavior—for example, for the child to stop putting others down, to get work done, or to end aggressive behavior. I might say, "I see that it's hard to discuss this right now. I'd like to help. Let's see if the rude comments stop."

Step 3. Understanding the cause of the problem

When the student and I agree that there's a problem (even if there's only a moderate or muffled agreement from the student) and we agree there's a need to solve it, we explore the *why* behind the problem. I suggest possible causes based on an understanding of children's need to belong, feel competent, and have choices. I'm also aware that confusion or frustration about academics may be an underlying cause. I often use "Could it be…" questions to initiate this discussion.

To Derek I said, "When I see kids go to the bathroom at a particular time every day, I think they want to avoid something they don't like or that's hard for them. Could it be that writing seems hard for you this year?"

Derek grinned and said, "Sort of. It's sort of hard."

Children don't always give a clear answer to our "Could it be…" questions. A "yeah, maybe," a slight nod, or sometimes a yes disguised as a shoulder shrug may be all we get. But those signals let us know it's okay to go on.

With Derek, I probed further to get at why writing was hard for him. As happens with many children, I needed to name several possible causes before he heard one that sounded right. "Could it be that writing is hard because you have trouble thinking of ideas? Or could it be that you know your main ideas, but you get confused about what words to use? Sometimes writers worry about the spelling or the handwriting. Could that be true for you?"

"Sometimes I can't think of the words I want," Derek replied.

Even when the cause of the behavior is very clear to me, I ask rather than assert. We gain children's confidence when we invite them to participate in the conversation. This confidence grows not because the teacher has brilliantly solved the mystery, but because the child was part of the process.

Step 4. Generating alternatives

"Do you think we could come up with some ways to help you remember the words you need?" I said next to Derek.

It often helps to list several alternatives before seizing upon one solution. In Derek's case, we decided together that he could brainstorm a list of words before starting a story. He could try some story-mapping exercises. Or he could jot down main ideas before starting to write.

Step 5. Choosing one strategy to try

Teacher-Child Problem Solving Conferences

The conference ends with an oral or written agreement to try one of the alternatives. With several possible strategies on the table, I asked Derek to choose one idea to try. He chose to try brainstorming a list of words.

Always, it's important that students choose an alternative that they believe will work, not one that just pleases the teacher. Over the next days and weeks, the student and teacher both take note of whether the problem they identified gets resolved. If not, they learn from the experience and return to the list of alternatives to make a better selection.

The strength of this problem solving approach is its openness to the child's perspective and ideas. We try to see children as they really are, exploring with them what they need in order to do better at school. Ironically the correct solution is not what's most important. What's most important is inviting the child into the conversation, searching together for solutions, and expressing faith in the child's ability to solve the problem.

REFERENCES

American Educational Research Association. 2004. "English Language Learners: Boosting Academic Achievement." *Research Points* (Winter): 1–4.

Brady, Kathryn, Mary Beth Forton, Deborah Porter, and Chip Wood. 2003. *Rules in School*. Greenfield, MA: Northeast Foundation for Children.

Charney, Ruth Sidney. 2002. *Teaching Children to Care: Classroom Management for Ethical and Academic Growth, K–8*. Greenfield, MA: Northeast Foundation for Children.

Crowe, Caltha. 2004. "Wonderful Wednesdays: Inviting Parents into Our Classroom Community." *Responsive Classroom Newsletter* (Fall): 4–5.

Cummins, Jim. 1991. "Interdependence of first- and second-language proficiency in bilingual children." In *Language Processing in Bilingual Children,* ed. E. Bialystok, 70–89. Cambridge: Cambridge University Press.

Davies, Anne, Caren Cameron, Colleen Politano, and Kathleen Gregory. 1992. *Together Is Better: Collaborative Assessment, Evaluation & Reporting*. Winnipeg, Canada: Peguis Publishers.

Delpit, Lisa. 1995. *Other People's Children: Cultural Conflicts in the Classroom*. New York: The New Press.

Delpit, Lisa, and Joanne Kilgour Dowdy, eds. 2002. *The Skin That We Speak*. New York: The New Press.

Fay, Kathleen, and Suzanne Whaley. 2004. *Becoming One Community: Reading & Writing with English Language Learners*. Portland, ME: Stenhouse Publishers.

Fitzgerald, J. 1995. "English-as-a-Second-Language Learners' Cognitive Reading Processes: A Review of Research in the United States." *Review of Educational Research* 65: 145–190.

Gordon, Debra. 2003. "Talking Points." *Teacher Magazine* (October): 8, 10.

Henderson, A.T., and Nancy Berla. 1995. *A New Generation of Evidence: The Family is Critical to Student Achievement*. Washington, DC: Center for Law and Education.

Henderson, A.T., and K.L. Mapp. 2002. *A New Wave of Evidence: The Impact of School, Family, and Community Connections on Student Achievement*. National Center for Family and Community Connections with Schools, Southwest Educational Development Laboratory.

Kriete, Roxann, with contributions by Lynn Bechtel. 2002. *The Morning Meeting Book*. Greenfield, MA: Northeast Foundation for Children.

Lawrence-Lightfoot, Sara. 2003. *The Essential Conversation: What Parents and Teachers Can Learn from Each Other*. New York: Random House.

National PTA. 2000. *Building Successful Partnerships: A Guide for Developing Parent and Family Involvement Programs*. Bloomington, IN: National Education Service.

Nieto, Sonia. 1999. *The Light in Their Eyes*. New York: Teachers College Press.

Routman, Regie. 1991. *Invitations: Changing as Teachers and Learners K–12*. Portsmouth, NH: Heinemann.

Routman, Regie. 2000. *Conversations: Strategies for Teaching, Learning, and Evaluating*. Portsmouth, NH: Heinemann.

Swap, Susan McAllister. 1993. *Developing Home School Partnerships*. New York: Teachers College Press.

Thomas, Wayne P., and Virginia P. Collier. 2002. *A National Study of School Effectiveness for Language Minority Students' Long-Term Academic Achievement*. Santa Cruz, CA: Center for Research on Education, Diversity and Excellence, University of California-Santa Cruz.

U.S. Census Bureau. 2000. *Table NP-T4-E. Projections of the Total Resident Population by 5-Year Age Groups, Race, and Hispanic Origin with Special Age Categories: Middle Series, 2016 to 2020*. Release date: January 13, 2000.

U.S. Census Bureau. June 18, 2003. *Table NA-EST2002-ASRO-03, National Population Estimates, Characteristics*. Source: Population Division, U.S. Census Bureau.

U.S. Census Bureau. September 26, 2003. *Poverty: 2002 Highlights*.

U.S. Department of Education. 2000–2001. *Language Backgrounds of Limited English Proficient (LEP) Students in the U.S. and Outlying Areas*.

Wells, Amy Stuart, Jennifer Jellison Holme, Anita Tijerina Revilla, and Awo Korantemaa Atanda. 2004. "How Desegregation Changed Us: The Effects of Racially Mixed Schools on Students and Society." In *In Search of Brown*. Cambridge: Harvard University Press, forthcoming.

Wood, Chip. 1997. *Yardsticks: Children in the Classroom Ages 4–14*. Greenfield, MA: Northeast Foundation for Children.

RECOMMENDED RESOURCES

Resources for Teachers

★ Included in References

Books and Articles

Brady, Kathryn, Mary Beth Forton, Deborah Porter, and Chip Wood. 2003. *Rules in School.* Greenfield, MA: Northeast Foundation for Children.★

Cartledge, Gwendolyn, with contributions by JoAnne Fellows Milburn. 1996. *Cultural Diversity and Social Skills Instruction: Understanding Ethnic and Gender Differences.* Champaign, IL: Research Press.

Charney, Ruth Sidney. 2002. *Teaching Children to Care: Classroom Management for Ethical and Academic Growth, K–8.* Greenfield, MA: Northeast Foundation for Children.★

Comer, James P., and Alvin F. Poussaint. 1992. *Raising Black Children.* New York: Plume Books.

Davies, Anne, Caren Cameron, Colleen Politano, and Kathleen Gregory. 1992. *Together Is Better: Collaborative Assessment, Evaluation & Reporting.* Winnipeg, Canada: Peguis Publishers.★

Delpit, Lisa. 1995. *Other People's Children: Cultural Conflicts in the Classroom.* New York: The New Press.★

Delpit, Lisa, and Joanne Kilgour Dowdy, eds. 2002. *The Skin That We Speak.* New York: The New Press.★

Fay, Kathleen, and Suzanne Whaley. 2004. *Becoming One Community: Reading & Writing with English Language Learners.* Portland, ME: Stenhouse Publishers.★

Gordon, Debra. 2003. "Talking Points." *Teacher Magazine* (October): 8, 10.★

Greenfield, Patricia M., and Rodney R. Cocking, eds. 1994. *Cross-Cultural Roots of Minority Child Development.* Hillsdale, NJ: Lawrence Erlbaum Associates.

Hale-Benson, Janice. 1986. *Black Children: Their Roots, Culture, and Learning Styles.* Baltimore: Johns Hopkins University Press.

Henderson, A.T., and Nancy Berla. 1995. *A New Generation of Evidence: The Family is Critical to Student Achievement.* Washington, DC: Center for Law and Education.★

Henderson, A.T., and K.L. Mapp. 2002. *A New Wave of Evidence: The Impact of School, Family, and Community Connections on Student Achievement.* National Center for Family and Community Connections with Schools, Southwest Educational Development Laboratory.★

Howard, Gary. 1999. *We Can't Teach What We Don't Know: White Teachers, Multiracial Schools.* New York: Teachers College Press.

Kriete, Roxann, with contributions by Lynn Bechtel. 2002. *The Morning Meeting Book.* Greenfield, MA: Northeast Foundation for Children.★

Ladson-Billings, Gloria. 2001. *Crossing Over to Canaan: The Journey of New Teachers in Diverse Classrooms.* San Francisco: Jossey-Bass Publishers.

Landsman, Julie. 2001. *A White Teacher Talks about Race.* Landham, MD: Scarecrow Press.

Lawrence-Lightfoot, Sara. 2003. *The Essential Conversation: What Parents and Teachers Can Learn from Each Other.* New York: Random House.★

Liston, Daniel P., and Kenneth M. Zeichner. 1996. *Culture and Teaching.* Mahwah, NJ: Lawrence Erlbaum Associates.

Lynch, Eleanor W., and Marci J. Hanson. 1998. *Developing Cross-Cultural Competence: A Guide for Working with Children and Their Families.* Baltimore, MD: Paul H. Brookes Publishing Co.

National PTA. 2000. *Building Successful Partnerships: A Guide for Developing Parent and Family Involvement Programs.* Bloomington, IN: National Education Service.★

Nieto, Sonia. 1999. *The Light in Their Eyes.* New York: Teachers College Press.★

Rogoff, Barbara. 2003. *The Cultural Nature of Human Development.* Reprint Edition. New York: Oxford University Press.

Swap, Susan McAllister. 1993. *Developing Home School Partnerships.* New York: Teachers College Press.★

Wells, Amy Stuart, Jennifer Jellison Holme, Anita Tijerina Revilla, and Awo Korantemaa Atanda. 2004. "How Desegregation Changed Us: The Effects of Racially Mixed Schools on Students and Society." In *In Search of Brown.* Cambridge: Harvard University Press, forthcoming.★

Wood, Chip. 1997. *Yardsticks: Children in the Classroom Ages 4–14.* Greenfield, MA: Northeast Foundation for Children.★

**Recommended
Resources**

Websites

Clearinghouse for English Language Acquisition & Language Instruction Educational Programs
www.ncela.gwu.edu

Funded by the U.S. Department of Education, this clearinghouse collects, analyzes, synthesizes, and disseminates information about language instruction programs for English language learners. It includes resources for teachers, prospective teachers, parents, community organizations, student researchers, Title I grantees, Title III grantees, and institutions of higher education.

Educator's Reference Desk[sm]
www.eduref.org

This umbrella site provides links to organizations, online communities, and other websites for a wide range of topics in education, including school-home collaboration, diversity in the classroom, background information on various ethnic cultures, parenting, and homework.

Harvard Family Research Project
www.gse.harvard.edu/hfrp/about.html

This project at the Harvard Graduate School of Education conducts research on the best ways of increasing school-home and school-community collaboration. This site offers research papers on the topic, links to other organizations, and links to many partnership models.

NCREL Parent Involvement Database of Promising Practices
www.ncrel.org/sdrs/pidata/pioover.htm

This database includes programs that the North Central Regional Educational Laboratory (NCREL) has found to have shown promise and accomplishment in raising the level of parent involvement in schools. Programs are categorized by geographic reach, grade range, and program focus or features.

Tolerance.org
www.tolerance.org

A project of the Southern Poverty Law Center, this website offers information to help teachers bridge cultures and teach children appreciation and respect for diversity. It provides daily news about groups and individuals fighting hate, guidebooks for adult and youth activists, practical resources for parents and teachers, entertaining and educational games for young children, and downloadable public service announcements.

Resources for Parents

Parents often ask teachers for suggestions on parenting books and other resources. Here are some that you might want to consider recommending:

Books

Brown, Scott. 2003. *How to Negotiate with Kids...even when you think you shouldn't.* New York: Penguin Books.

Faber, Adele, and Elaine Mazlish. 1995. *How To Talk So Kids Can Learn at Home and in School.* New York: Simon and Schuster.

Nelsen, Jane. 1996. *Positive Discipline.* New York: Random House.

Nelsen, Jane. 1999. *Positive Time-Out and Over 50 Ways to Avoid Power Struggles in the Home and the Classroom.* Roseville, CA: Prima Publishing.

Recommended Resources

Websites

The Collaborative for Academic, Social, and Emotional Learning
www.casel.org

Easy-to-use information on nurturing children's social and emotional learning. A section of the site is devoted to information for parents on how they can support their children's social and emotional learning at home.

National PTA
www.pta.org

Tips, fact sheets, and articles, useful to parents and teachers, on a wide range of topics related to parenting and school-home collaboration.

School Success Info.org
www.schoolsuccessinfo.org

Highly practical tips for parents on how to work with their children's school and how to support their children's learning at home.

INDEX OF SAMPLE LETTERS AND FORMS

ABOUT THE AUTHORS

Carol Davis has worked as a teacher, counselor, and consultant with children of all ages and their parents in rural, suburban, and urban settings throughout the U.S. She received her BS in elementary education from Miami University in Oxford, Ohio, and her MEd in school counseling from the University of Cincinnati. Currently, Carol is a consulting teacher for Northeast Foundation for Children (NEFC), leading workshops and coaching teachers in their classrooms. In addition, she is a school counselor in the Centerville Public Schools in Dayton, Ohio.

Alice Yang has been in the writing and editing field for twenty years. She began her career as a newspaper reporter before deciding to work for organizations devoted to children's well-being. She was a writer for the Children's Defense Fund, among other places, before joining NEFC's editorial staff. She is currently manager of publications at NEFC. Alice has a BA in communication from Stanford University and an MA in English from the University of Maryland.

ABOUT THE
RESPONSIVE CLASSROOM® APPROACH

This book grew out of the work of Northeast Foundation for Children (NEFC) and an approach to teaching known as the *Responsive Classroom* approach. Developed by classroom teachers, this approach consists of highly practical strategies for integrating social and academic learning throughout the school day. Seven beliefs underlie this approach:

1. The social curriculum is as important as the academic curriculum.

2. How children learn is as important as what they learn: Process and content go hand in hand.

3. The greatest cognitive growth occurs through social interaction.

4. There is a specific set of social skills that children need to learn and practice in order to be successful academically and socially: cooperation, assertion, responsibility, empathy, and self-control.

5. Knowing the children we teach—individually, culturally, and developmentally—is as important as knowing the content we teach.

6. Knowing the families of the children we teach and encouraging their participation is as important as knowing the children we teach.

7. How we, the adults at school, work together to accomplish our shared mission is as important as our individual competence: Lasting change begins with the adult community.

**More information and guidance on the
Responsive Classroom approach are available through:**

Publications and Resources

- Books, videos, and audios for elementary school educators

- Website with articles and other information:
  www.responsiveclassroom.org

- Free quarterly newsletter for educators

Professional Development Opportunities

- One-day and weeklong workshops for teachers

- Classroom consultations and other services at individual schools and school districts

- Multifaceted professional development for administrators and all staff at schools wishing to implement the *Responsive Classroom* approach school-wide

For details, contact:

RESPONSIVE CLASSROOM
85 Avenue A, Suite 204   P.O. Box 718
Turners Falls, MA 01376-0718
Phone 800-360-6332 or 413-863-8288
Fax 877-206-3952
www.responsiveclassroom.org

The Morning Meeting Book
By Roxann Kriete
with contributions by Lynn Bechtel

For K–8 teachers (2002) 228 pages ISBN 978-1-892989-09-3

Use Morning Meeting in your classroom to build community, increase students' investment in learning, and improve academic and social skills. This book features:

■ *Step-by-step guidelines for holding Morning Meeting* ■ *A chapter on Morning Meeting in middle schools* ■ *45 greetings and 66 group activities* ■ *Frequently asked questions and answers*

The First Six Weeks of School
By Paula Denton and Roxann Kriete

For K–6 teachers (2000) 232 pages ISBN 978-1-892989-04-8

Structure the first weeks of school to lay the groundwork for a productive year of learning.

■ *Guidelines for the first six weeks, including daily plans for the first three weeks for grades K–2, grades 3–4, and grades 5–6* ■ *Ideas for building community, teaching routines, introducing engaging curriculum, fostering autonomy* ■ *Games, activities, greetings, songs, read-alouds, and resources especially useful during the early weeks of school*

Classroom Spaces That Work
By Marlynn K. Clayton with Mary Beth Forton

For K–6 teachers (2001) 192 pages ISBN 978-1-892989-05-5

Create a physical environment that is welcoming, well suited to the needs of students and teachers, and conducive to social and academic excellence.

■ *Practical ideas for arranging furniture* ■ *Suggestions for selecting and organizing materials* ■ *Ideas for creating displays* ■ *Guidelines for setting up a meeting area* ■ *Tips for making the space healthy*

Rules in School

By Kathryn Brady, Mary Beth Forton,
Deborah Porter, and Chip Wood

For K–8 teachers (2003) 272 pages ISBN 978-1-892989-10-9

Establish a calm, safe learning environment and teach children self-discipline with this approach to classroom rules.

- *Guidelines for creating rules with students based on their hopes and dreams for school*
- *Steps in modeling and role playing the rules* ■ *How to reinforce the rules through language*
- *Using logical consequences when rules are broken* ■ *Suggestions for teaching children to live by the rules outside the classroom*

Learning Through Academic Choice

By Paula Denton, EdD

For K–6 teachers (2005) 224 pages ISBN 978-1-892989-14-7

Enhance students' learning with this powerful tool for structuring lessons and activities.

- *Information on building a strong foundation for Academic Choice* ■ *Step-by-step look at Academic Choice in action* ■ *Practical advice for creating an Academic Choice lesson plan*
- *Many ideas for Academic Choice activities*

Parents and Teachers Working Together

By Carol Davis and Alice Yang

For K–6 teachers (2005) 232 pages ISBN 978-1-892989-15-4

Build school-home cooperation and involve parents in ways that support their children's learning.

- *Working with diverse family cultures* ■ *Building positive relationships in the early weeks of school* ■ *Keeping in touch all year long* ■ *Involving parents in classroom life, including parents who can't physically come to school* ■ *Problem-solving with parents*